grace
by the Cup

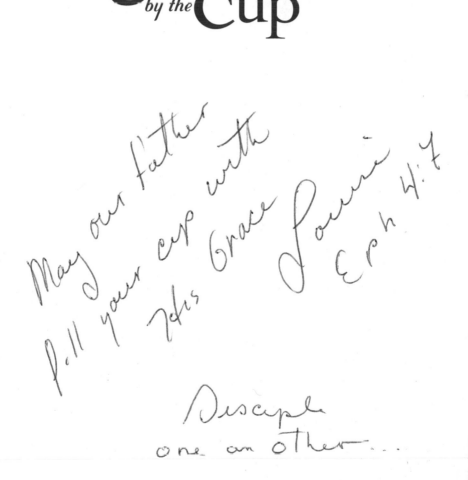

May our Father
fill your cup with
this Grace

Lonnie
Eph 4:7

Disciple
one an other...

grace by the Cup

A Break from the Daily Grind

Louise Bergmann DuMont

Fleming H. Revell
A Division of Baker Book House Co
Grand Rapids, Michigan 49516

© 2003 by Louise Bergmann DuMont

Published by Fleming H. Revell
a division of Baker Book House Company
P.O. Box 6287, Grand Rapids, MI 49516-6287

Printed in the United States of America

Published in association with the literary agency of Janet Kobobel Grant, Books & Such, 4788 Carissa Ave., Santa Rosa, CA 95405.

Library of Congress Cataloging-in-Publication Data
DuMont, Louise Bergmann, 1952–
     Grace by the cup : a break from the daily grind / Louise Bergmann
DuMont.
           p.   cm.
     ISBN 0-8007-5888-9 (pbk.)
     1. Christian women—Prayer-books and devotions—English. 2. Coffee
habit—Miscellanea. I. Title.
BV4844.D86 2003
242'.643—dc21   2003010531

Unless otherwise noted, Scripture is taken from the New Revised Standard Version of the Bible, copyright 1989 by the Division of Christian Education of the National Council of the Churches of Christ in the USA. Used by permission.

Scripture marked ASV is taken from the *American Standard Version* of the Bible.

Scripture marked KJV is taken from the King James Version of the Bible.

Scripture marked NASB is taken from the NEW AMERICAN STANDARD BIBLE ®. Copyright © The Lockman Foundation 1960, 1962, 1963, 1968, 1971, 1972, 1973, 1975, 1977, 1995. Used by permission.

Scripture marked NIV is taken from the HOLY BIBLE, NEW INTERNATIONAL VERSION®. NIV®. Copyright © 1973, 1978, 1984 by International Bible Society. Used by permission of Zondervan. All rights reserved.

Scripture marked NKJV is taken from the New King James Version. Copyright © 1979, 1980, 1982 by Thomas Nelson, Inc. Used by permission. All rights reserved.

Scripture marked NLT is taken from the *Holy Bible,* New Living Translation, copyright © 1996. Used by permission of Tyndale House Publishers, Inc., Wheaton, IL 60189. All rights reserved.

Scripture marked RSV is taken from the Revised Standard Version of the Bible, copyright 1946, 1952, 1971 by the Division of Christian Education of the National Council of the Churches of Christ in the USA. Used by permission.

Scripture marked TEV is taken from the Good News Bible, Today's English Version. Copyright © American Bible Society 1966, 1971, 1976, 1992. Used by permission.

This book is dedicated to:
Lisa Wiener and CWG (the Christian Writers' Group),
whose
scholarship set in motion so many of God's blessings,
and
Jason Mitchener, webmaster www.crosshome.com,
who gave a wannabe a break.

Many thanks to Lauren Cooper
for her unparalleled proofing and editing skills,
and
last, but certainly not least, thanks to my husband and
my kids for allowing me to write all that I did.
You guys are the best. . . .

contents

1

taking a break

The office buzzed with its usual midmorning activity as I filled the coffee carafe with cold water.

"You making a fresh pot?" a voice from behind me asked. I nodded as a woman I didn't recognize slipped into a nearby chair to wait.

I continued with my task, measuring out the coffee and flipping on the switch before turning toward the hallway from which I'd come.

"Aren't you going to wait for the coffee?" the woman questioned with obvious surprise.

"My desk is just around the corner from here. I'll be back when it's done," I replied over my shoulder.

The quizzical look on her face made me cringe. This woman obviously did not understand what it was like to have stacks of projects waiting for completion, lists of phone messages to return, and files upon files of material calling for her personal attention. I sighed as I dropped into my chair and plunged into paperwork, forcing from my mind the scent drifting from the dripping pot just down the hall.

A few moments later a soft clearing of the throat made me look up. "The coffee's done. Join me for a cup."

Logic dictated that I counter with a polite negative response . . . but there was something about her request. It was more of a declaration than an offer. Instead of saying no, the word "Sure!" popped out of my mouth.

A grin spread across her face and she led the way back to the coffeepot. I poured myself a cup of strong black coffee and moved to a nearby table for two where my new friend had already taken a seat.

During our conversation I discovered that she too was a coffee connoisseur, and we formed a quick bond discussing the merits of Hawaiian coffee beans. Before long we'd drifted into office small talk, finished our coffee, and were ready to return to work.

"Thanks for joining me. You feel better?" she asked with a knowing smile.

"Yes, thanks. I'm glad you talked me into taking a break," I responded.

As we walked back toward my desk, she added, "There are a lot of things I don't have time to do, but I've found that taking an occasional break is time well spent."

What wise counsel, I thought as I tackled the stack of files on my desk with renewed vigor. Even Jesus took an occasional break from the crowds and encouraged his disciples to do the same. Since that day, I've made a point of taking coffee breaks. The more work I have, the more I need to take a break.

He said to them, "Come away to a deserted place all by yourselves and rest a while." For many were coming and going, and they had no leisure even to eat.

Mark 6:31

2

the hawk

A large hawk was perched not three feet from the ledge of my office window. He stared at me, unflinching, with eyes as dark as Mississippi mud. Periodically he would scan the surrounding area as if to point out that he was not terribly concerned with my presence. I estimated him to be a good twenty inches tall; he sat so close to my desk that I could see the rise and fall of the feathers on his chest.

I called out to others down the hall, imploring them to come quickly but quietly to my window. A dozen coworkers gathered around to watch the magnificent bird sitting regally upon one of the parking lot floodlights extending from our building. Once or twice the hawk flexed his shoulder muscles, spreading his wings for us to "ooh" and "aah" over his strength. For almost ten minutes he watched us and we watched him. Then, ever so nonchalantly, he took flight, returning once again to wherever hawks go when they fly away from their gawkers.

One by one, the group gathered near my window retreated to their respective desks, leaving behind a strange scent of regret and an aura that reflected their reluctance to leave. I was having some trouble getting myself back to work as well, so I did the only logical thing—I headed to the cafeteria for a late cup of coffee. I knew the strong brew would help me gather my thoughts and sort out the questions arising from our unexpected visitor.

Why were we all so drawn to this creature? Why did we feel the need to remain even after he flew off? The answers that came were simple, but their implications were profound.

While sipping my coffee I drew two conclusions. Few individuals have an opportunity to get close to one of these magnificent birds. He was so different from the common sparrow or pigeon we were accustomed to, and we were drawn to his strangeness. Secondly, we were impressed by his unusual strength, power, and regal bearing—all things humans strive for.

By the time I poured my second cup of coffee, I'd reflected on a number of other things. Unbelievers are drawn to Christlike behavior for the same reason the group was compelled to watch the hawk. Genuine Christians are "different" from the world. Unbelievers may inspect them with some caution, but they *are* drawn to watch them. Such Christians are vastly different from the rest of the world—different in the best sort of way.

This thought made me wonder: Do I as a Christian occasionally flex my muscles and show unbelievers the strength God put into my wings? Or do I only fly in the safety of other believers, displaying my prowess for nothing more than self-gratification?

Do others see my regal bearing and my access to the King of Kings? Or do they see a common individual more interested in winning an argument than in finding solutions to difficult problems that keep others in bondage?

What scent do I leave with my colleagues and family when I leave a room? Do they miss my calming presence, my wisdom, my uplifting words and spirit? Do others linger for just a moment after I'm gone, hoping for my return?

12

Watching that hawk made me realize that unbelievers do examine Christians' lives. I pray they will long for the "difference" they see in me.

So if anyone is in Christ, there is a new creation: everything old has passed away; see, everything has become new!

2 Corinthians 5:17

3

cracker box gifts

I stared at the ill-wrapped package presented to me. Although an attempt had been made to smooth the paper, the wrapping was slightly crumpled. Remnants of old tape gave strong evidence that this was not the first package the paper had covered. The ribbon was made of a bright and cheery fabric, but its frayed edges showed signs of wear.

I looked up and smiled at the anxious shining eyes before me. The wrinkles around their corners were deep and became even more so when they returned my smile.

"Thank you so much for this gift," I said, "but you really didn't have to do this."

"I know . . ." replied the slightly unsteady voice. "But you've done so much for me, I just wanted to give you a little something."

I smiled again, but this time it was to hide the bit of guilt I felt creeping into my chest. The help I offered was nothing extraordinary. It was simply what was necessary to pull together our monthly senior citizen program . . . and to my discredit it was not always performed with the most generous heart.

"Aren't you going to open it?" my senior friend continued, a hint of concern entering her quavering voice.

"Oh, of course!" I responded, swiftly removing the ribbon and tearing away the paper.

The gift box underneath the paper was interestingly fashioned by cutting away the center portion of a saltine cracker box and using its opposite ends as the base and lid of the box.

"I could not find a box that would fit the gift, so I had to make this one," the elderly woman said apologetically.

"I think it was a great idea," I responded, watching relief fill her tired eyes.

Gingerly separating the two portions of the cracker box, I lifted out a newspaper-wrapped object. From its shape and feel, I knew what the paper held even before removing it. A grin spread across my face as I carefully disengaged the gift from its cover.

"A coffee mug! You're so sweet. You know how much I enjoy my coffee, and this mug is just what I needed." The mug's flowery picture was not something I would choose for myself, but I knew this woman owned little. I surmised that the well-used mug was most likely one she'd bought at a yard sale.

Then came the surprise.

"I know it isn't new," she apologized, "but I wanted you to have this. My husband gave it to me many years ago." The woman lovingly took the mug from me and with shaky hands turned it over to expose the underside. There in black permanent marker were the words *Proverbs 16:16.*

"I've read that verse every day since he gave me this gift. Each time I washed it along with our breakfast dishes, I was reminded that I needed to spend more time in the Word of God. The other day I felt the Lord calling me to pass it to you." When she passed back the mug, I felt as if she were offering me a great inheritance. No longer was my mind on the wrinkled paper, the faded ribbon, or the cracker box. This was a precious gift indeed.

I kept that mug on my desk at work for years, as a reminder of God's priorities. Last year I moved from the second to the third floor, and the mug unexpectedly disappeared. I missed its presence so much that I created a small sign that now stands next to my computer. It says:

How much better to get wisdom than gold! To get understanding is to be chosen rather than silver.

Proverbs 16:16

My friend is no longer with us, but I know that while on this earth she lived that verse. I hope the same can be said for me someday.

4

waiting

Clink, clink, clink . . . I dropped the coins into the hotel coffee machine with great anticipation. As my eyes searched for the cappuccino button, my mind envisioned walking along the nearby bay, beverage in hand. The morning was quiet and my life was in perfect order.

Swoosh . . . the sound of gushing beverage abruptly returned me to the present when the *pop* of the cup entering the dispenser did not precede it. Turning my attention to the machine, I watched foamy milk shooting directly into the disposal tray where the cup should have sat. I grabbed a paper cup from a nearby stack and quickly thrust it into the appropriate slot. Then I watched as the last remnant of the foam squirted into the bottom of the container. The air filled with defeated silence as I reached for the nearly bare cup.

"No, don't!" admonished a voice from behind me. "It's not done."

I pulled back my hand, and at that moment the machine began another song. This time it was more of a *chug, whirr, chug.*

It began to add hot black coffee to the foam already in the cup, and the scent filled my heart with joy.

"I did the same thing the other day," the kindly gentleman said over my shoulder. "Only no one warned me, so I pulled the cup out and never caught a drop of coffee."

I clutched my precious beverage with both hands, took a sip, and smiled gratefully.

The next morning while making a small pot of coffee in my hotel room I rethought the prior day's incident. This time I did not have to worry about whether or not the cup would be ready when I poured the beverage. I was prepared.

Yet it made me wonder. How many times was God ready to give me a blessing only to find my mind was elsewhere and my cup not ready for what he had to offer me? Then there were times when I pulled my cup away from God before he had the opportunity to give me the best portion of a blessing. I often find myself impatient and ready to accept only a bit of foam rather than wait for the wonderful brew he wants to share. The Word warns me to keep my cup at the ready. When I heed the warning, I am always blessed.

Therefore the LORD waits to be gracious to you; therefore he will rise up to show mercy to you. For the LORD is a God of justice; blessed are all those who wait for him.

Isaiah 30:18

5

frogs and ducks

They are everywhere—fat ones, skinny ones, short ones, tall ones. Some are embellished with profound sayings and flowery mottoes, while others sport cartoon characters or advertise trendy products.

Coffee mugs are a unique art form. Any serious coffee drinker will confirm that the mug you drink from is almost as important as the beverage itself.

Personally I find a mug with a thin lip most comfortable. I also want a handle I can get a real grip on. No delicate china cup for me, thanks. My mug also needs to be easy to clean. I learned about that the hard way some years ago when I promised my kids that they could pick out new mugs of their own.

"Mom, p-l-e-a-s-e can I have this one?" my oldest child pleaded.

"J. C., don't you like the one over here?" I asked, directing my son to a nearby shelf. "It has a picture of those turtle guys you like so much, see?"

"But this one has a *frog* on the bottom of the cup, Mom," he said as if this was all the explanation that was needed.

I examined the mug he held out to me. Inside the mug was a cute little ceramic frog, firmly attached to a bright green lily pad.

"And look, Mom," my son continued. "Here is one with a duck! We can get this one for Alan!" His outstretched hand now held a second mug. This one held a small yellow duck sitting in the midst of a puddle.

His brother looked up from where he sat inside the shopping cart. "Ducky!" he shouted with obvious glee. My decision was made.

The kids loved their new mugs! Milk and juice were cheerfully consumed in order to greet frog and ducky. But cleaning these mugs was not a pleasant experience at all. A gentle, long-bristled bottle brush needed to be carefully maneuvered under the edges of the lily pad and puddle where lingering chocolate syrup or orange juice pulp remained after every use. No quick swoosh, swoosh of a sponge would be sufficient here.

Sometimes I feel my life is a little like those mugs. I've adorned it with so many unnecessary frogs, ducks, lily pads, and puddles. God loves me and won't allow old deposits to accumulate in the nooks of my life. He constantly scrubs to get the gunk out from under things so he can supply me with the fresh and healthy substance I need to quench my spiritual thirst. I stubbornly insist that I like my little frogs and continue to enjoy them even though they may get in the way of the healthy "best" that God wants to offer me.

I'm so glad that God is persistent in scrubbing away the unhealthy residue even when I'm reluctant to relinquish my bad habits.

Have mercy on me, O God, according to your unfailing love; . . . Wash away all my iniquity, and cleanse me from my sin.

Psalm 51:1–2 NIV

6

presentations

I could feel myself fighting back the tears that threatened to escape underneath my already foggy glasses. Rather than explain a fit of unrestrained sobbing to my coworkers, I bridled my emotions and directed my feet toward the strongest cup of coffee our cafeteria could offer. Secretly I hoped that I would burn my tongue on the scorching black brew, so I could justify my tears. When this didn't happen, I returned to my desk with the tepid cup while contemplating my still-brewing emotions.

I had come in early that morning and taken a quick break to read an e-mail message from an old friend. For a long time she'd been encouraged to put her Christian testimony into words. Recent circumstances finally allowed her to do just that.

I was totally unprepared for the effect her story would have on me. I'd known Eleanor for most of my adult life. We'd raised our sons side by side. We'd spent hundreds of hours digging deep into God's Word, sharing and comparing notes, crying and rejoicing with each other. She was there for me when I so desperately needed a friend, and I tried to be her friend when she needed one as well. Married to a Jewish man, she provided insight to Scripture that I could never have dreamed of. As our infants grew into children, I provided transportation to nursery school for her son, and she made me wonderful matzo ball soup and potato latkes. I definitely got the better part of that deal!

Over hundreds of cups of coffee, I learned bits about her very difficult childhood and teen years. But in all our years of friendship, she never complained or dwelled on the past. Maybe that is why I never got the complete picture back then. Now her story sat in black and white, laid out before me like the front page of the *Wall Street Journal.*

While reading the first two pages of her testimony, I wondered if I was reading some stranger's story. Could all of this really have happened to my friend? Then I reached the part where Eleanor met a woman she obviously considered to be very special. The woman she wrote about sounded so strong, so willing to share the gospel. She seemed to know just what to say and what to do. This person was someone I wanted to know and, moreover, someone I wanted to emulate. Then the name of the person hit me — my friend was writing about me! My tears began to flow.

My version of Eleanor's story was totally different. The confident and fearless woman she spoke of was nothing more than a scared girl who loved the Lord but felt inadequate to share any words of wisdom. Only a short while after meeting Eleanor, I knew she was ready to hear God's truth. She came right out and asked me to tell her about Jesus. You can't get more ready than that! After I made a lame attempt at presenting the gospel, I directed Eleanor to a wonderful evangelical television program. This was not because I wanted to reinforce my words, but because I was afraid I'd botched the job. I could count on the program imparting the gospel in a clear and straightforward way. She watched that program and accepted Christ that same day.

I feel privileged that God used me to bring Eleanor and others to know him. I've given many presentations in my life, but none so poorly as the one given to my friend. I am awed that the magnificent God I serve can use even my inadequate attempts to create something wonderful.

See, now is the acceptable time; see, now is the day of salvation!

2 Corinthians 6:2

7

right place, right time

The sky was still the color of pitch as I stumbled toward my car mumbling something about it being *very* early. I was unable to make a pot of coffee before leaving the house, so it was taking extra effort to gather my thoughts. Putting the final touches on a homemade Christmas gift had kept me awake into the early hours. Then, on this midweek morning, I was up with the roosters, taking my youngest to Breakfast Club, his Wednesday morning high school prayer meeting.

"You okay, Mom? You look tired," my son Tim asked as he neatly slid his gangly sixteen-year-old frame into the front of the car.

"Grumph . . . brumble . . . hurmph . . ." I muttered.

"Yeah, me too," he replied without batting an eye.

We drove in the silent dark, stopping to pick up the other four kids willing to brave the wee hours. I dropped them off at the diner with little more than another grunt or two and then headed to the office with less than exuberant enthusiasm.

The sun was just beginning to peek over the horizon, and the mist that gently enfolds our dark mountains had begun to fade. On my left, where the sun was rising, the valley lay still shrouded in its night cloak. To my right rose the cliffs of jagged rock through which the highway was cut. All this was not unusual to me since I drove this stretch of road every day, but on this morning God had a surprise in store.

The first rays of the sun struck the rough rocks with force, lighting them with a magnificent and unexpected brilliance. Numerous trails of water trickling from the top of the mountain now glistened like strings of dancing diamonds, and the portions of the cliff containing iron ore glowed red and gold like carefully polished brass on a candelabra.

I gulped for air. No double espresso could have jolted me awake as quickly as this amazing sight. My soul began to cry out to God in response to this glorious display of his handiwork. The damp darkness of the night gave way to the brightness of the day, and along with it flew my dismal attitude.

"Oh, God, please let me remember this moment the next time my world crumbles into the dark," I prayed.

God ever so gently responded to my heart, "Child, I placed you here in this car, at this place, on this day, at this moment, and raised the sun's rays to strike the mountain at just the right angle at this time. I did this for you because it is what you needed today. When you are in need again, I will respond with exactly what you need on that day, in that place, at that time."

I don't remember much about the rest of the drive to work. I do remember that what I saw only took an instant in time, but its effect on my life continues. If I close my eyes, I can still conjure the feeling of that moment. God bent down and touched me through his creation. Since then I've been comforted many times by God's hand. Each time is unique, especially made for my need at that moment.

Sometimes I wonder if anyone else saw what I saw that morning. I imagine that many people drove down that highway oblivious to the beauty in front of them. May I always allow my spirit to be sensitive to his touch and his timing.

Thus says the LORD: "In an acceptable time I have heard you, And in the day of salvation I have helped you."

Isaiah 49:8 NKJV

8

the boss

I recently saw a movie trailer that caught my attention. In the ad a mob boss turns to his subordinate and in a controlled but deadly voice announces, *"I'm* the boss around here!"

Now my husband and I laugh every time we hear this line because it reminds us of our second son. When he was younger, he frequently taunted his older brother by declaring, "Hey, you're not the boss of me! I can do whatever I want!"

Now, I'm not sure I would ever *shout* those angry words at God, but I wonder how often my heavenly Father has heard me whisper those words under my breath. I don't consider myself a control freak, but I admit that I dislike situations where things are out of my control. At times I can almost hear God sigh when my defiant "You're not the boss of me! I can do whatever I want!" reaches his ears.

God wants to help me through life, but he will not force me to submit to what he knows is best for me. He gives me the free will to go down whatever path I choose, and he sadly allows me to experience the consequences that go along with some of my choices.

When I stumble over life's cracks and come running back to him, like the loving Father that he is, he pulls me onto his lap and kisses my hurts. Then he ever so gently asks me if I'm ready to let him lead me instead. The path he takes me down often seems rougher than the one I would choose for myself, but amazingly I don't fall nearly as much. He always walks in front of me and firmly holds my hand. So long as I don't fight his solid grip, I'm okay. Leaving him in control is the key, because I can walk anywhere once he's cleared the path in front of me.

Sipping my lovely black brew during my morning devotional time, I think about all the people who believe they are their own masters. In truth, they are only fooling themselves. We all serve one thing or another. Some people are slaves to their jobs, while others are slaves to their passions. Many are slaves to the bitterness they carry around from some past experience, or to earthly self-preservation and material possessions. The Bible says, "No [one] can serve two masters" (Luke 16:13). Every day we make a choice to let something rule what we do. I would much rather serve a loving heavenly Father who has my best interests at heart than the anger or bitterness I've allowed to seethe within myself.

Whom do *I* want my boss to be? Jesus Christ—without question. His words comfort me when I'm hurt, make me strong when I'm weak, and correct me when I'm wrong. He rejoices with me when I'm happy and continually cheers my accomplishments. He loves me more than I could ever love him in return—so much so that he was willing to die to give me possession of his inheritance in heaven. Yes, Jesus is "the boss of me," for sure!

"As the Father loved Me, I also have loved you; abide in My love. . . . These things I have spoken to you, that My joy may remain in you, and that your joy may be full. This is My commandment, that you love one another as I have loved you. Greater love has no one than this, than to lay down one's life for his friends."

John 15:9, 11–13 NKJV

9

newfound wisdom

Given the choice of pain or pleasure, which will you choose? As a human being, I want to choose pleasure over pain. But God's Word reveals that he has a purpose in all things. Does God have a use for pain? As strange as it may seem to some, I believe he does.

A while back I had a Friday morning appointment to have my upper wisdom teeth extracted. The dentist said that I would be "uncomfortable," but that I should have no trouble returning to work on Monday. I knew what he really meant—I was to endure a weekend of pain, and by Monday I'd be glad to go to work just to get my mind off of it.

The anesthetic worked well, the extraction went smoothly, and I felt no pain during the procedure. In no time at all I was minus two wisdom teeth but much nearer to genuine wisdom than I realized.

I'm past the worst part. The rest should be easy, I thought as I approached the reception desk.

The nurse recommended that I get my pain prescription filled immediately and take my first dose before the local anesthetic wore off.

"Great plan!" I exclaimed with as much enthusiasm and gusto as my numb mouth would allow. "That way I can expect to be totally pain free the whole time, right?" She just smiled.

I did exactly as I was told. I filled the prescription immediately and took my first dose as soon as I arrived home. There was only one little problem. Independent of the dental surgery, and unknown to me, I'd developed a bladder infection, and the codeine that I was taking to alleviate the pain of the dental work was getting rid of *all* of my body's pain.

Anticipating my return to work on Monday, I decided to wean myself off the codeine on Sunday. With no painkiller left in my system that evening, I became acutely aware that something else was wrong. I knew it wasn't just my assailed gums that hurt—I hurt all over. I had a fever, and my body ached so terribly that even my hair follicles seemed to radiate pain. I spent most of Monday morning in the bathroom, praying that my doctor would get in early. Despite the fact that I would have done almost anything to get rid of the pain, something told me *not* to take any more pain relievers. I needed to tell the doctor exactly what was wrong. How was I going to do that if the pain was masked?

God's plan was becoming clear.

I got in to see the doctor that afternoon. He examined me, ran a few quick tests, and prescribed a broad-spectrum antibiotic. Within an hour of filling that prescription, I felt a whole lot better. This time I knew I was getting rid of the cause of the problem, not just the pain. I suddenly was reminded of a speaker at our church earlier that month—a counselor for a drug rehabilitation program. He told us that most drug addicts don't die from an overdose; they die from secondary causes. When an addict comes down with the flu or is undernourished, he doesn't feel the flu bug or the ache in his stomach; he feels nothing. The flu often turns into pneumonia, and the hunger turns into starvation. The drugs take away pain indiscriminately, and the addict is unaware that his life is threatened.

God created an emergency brake in our body and called it *pain*. Back when Adam and Eve lived in a perfect garden, there was no need for pain. But when sin came into the world, the Father needed to protect Adam and Eve. They could no longer be trusted to do what was good and right simply because God asked them to. Their fear of pain kept them from hurting themselves and repeating mistakes.

I am glad God allowed me to feel the pain of my infection before it became too serious to treat. But will I be that wise when sin is infecting my life? Or will I administer conscience painkillers, so I can ignore the sin? I pray that his mercy will allow my pain to turn me from sin.

The LORD has appeared of old to me, saying: "Yes, I have loved you with an everlasting love; Therefore with lovingkindness I have drawn you."

Jeremiah 31:3 NKJV

10

gas station coffee

Dawn was still hours away when we put the last bags into our already crammed minivan. We were off to deliver our son to college and had a good ten hours of highway driving ahead of us. I was already straining for a cup of coffee, but my husband, John, suggested we put a few miles on the road before stopping for breakfast.

As we passed Goldberg's Bagel Shop on the other side of our town, I wanted to press my nose up against the car window like a homeless waif looking into a bakery shop window. Instead I simply murmured, "They make the *best* bagels there . . . and their coffee . . . hmm . . ." I sighed as John drove past, ignoring my pathetic plea.

A hundred miles later, my husband pulled into a gas station. "You want to get a cup of coffee and a bagel while I fill up the car?" he asked, pointing toward a sign that offered the same.

"Sure thing!" I replied, bolting out of the car as fast as my stiffened limbs would allow. While my husband filled the gas tank, I would fill my languid body with some much-needed coffee. I could already imagine the warmth of the cup in my hands as I headed for the service counter. I first ordered the bagels, but the clerk was unable to slice through them even after trying three different knives. She seemed grateful when I told her to forget the bagels and just get us coffee. Hurrying to the car, I did not even wait for the door to close behind me before I tore back the plastic lid that topped my cup. My husband just rolled his eyes, fastened his seat belt, and calmly declared, "Watch out. It'll be hot."

I paused only long enough to smile patiently and then took a large gulp. Gagging and sputtering coffee everywhere, I yelped and grabbed for a handful of napkins. This was not coffee. It was some form of swamp water with a bit of motor oil mixed in for texture.

"I warned you it would be hot," my husband said, frowning.

"The fact that it's hot is the only good thing about it," I blurted. "This is the worst coffee I've ever tasted. They have a lot of nerve even calling this stuff coffee!"

He glanced in my direction as I once again took a gulp. "If it's so bad, why are you drinking it?" he asked with his usual maddening logic.

"Because it's all I have," I grumbled, taking a smaller sip.

Then John shot me a truly perplexed look. "In another couple of miles we can get fresh coffee. You don't *have* to drink this if you don't want to."

The cup froze inches from my lips as I pondered the profound choice presented to me. "You're right, John. This stuff is not worth the effort it takes to swallow it. I'll wait until we stop again."

Miles later, my husband dozed in the passenger seat while I drove, pondering the delicious gourmet coffee now sitting in my cup holder and the swill I'd forced down earlier. Few would call me an especially patient person, but even I profess to know that there are things in life worth waiting for. My current situation was not just about coffee . . . it was about patience and waiting for God's best.

I'm glad that God, like a good father, won't give me even the best of things before the time is right. Settling for "gas station" coffee or other "second bests" is no longer for me. I've decided to wait for the gourmet brew that my King serves.

"If you then, being evil, know how to give good gifts to your children, how much more will your Father who is in heaven give good things to those who ask Him!"

Matthew 7:11 NKJV

11

vocabulary

The week our church holds its vacation Bible school is one of my favorite times of the year. It takes me out of my adult world of paper clips and file folders and back to the carefree days of my childhood. VBS music was made for hand clapping and toe tapping. The sound of kids playing tag in the warm air and the smell of watermelon all mingle with serious Bible discussions and children who giggle over clay crafts gone awry.

Even the first day can prove interesting. I recall a conversation between one of our teachers and two boys waiting for their mother to complete their registration forms.

"You two seem to be having fun," the teacher remarked to the older of the two as she watched them giggle and squirm in anticipation. "Is the young man next to you a relation of yours?"

In all seriousness the boy turned to her and replied, "He's no relation; he's my brother."

We grin at this misunderstanding of her words, but upon closer reflection I am reminded of the many times that I respond to God's requests with total confidence—only to find out that I've totally misunderstood his words.

As a young adult I remember wanting desperately to do "big things" for God. Not so patiently, I waited for him to inform the world that I would now be in charge of things. The Bible says he will give us *the desire of our heart.* If I had the desire to do big things for God, it must mean that God had big plans for me! My logic seemed infallible.

There was one problem—my limited vocabulary. Months of unproductive waiting allowed me to ponder God's definition of "big." My contemplation led to some humbling conclusions and a key decision. Then and there I made up my mind to simply do whatever task God set in my path. No longer did it matter if I thought the job was noteworthy or trivial. I washed dishes at a senior program, prepared Sunday school crafts, washed pews, cooked meals for shut-in families, wiped runny noses, and cleaned toilets. Amazingly enough, I did all of this with a big smile. I was beginning to see that these *were* big things in God's eyes.

I admit that I now hold positions that seem to have more authority than those I just listed . . . but not one of them is any more precious to God than taking a turn in the church nursery. Even the most meager tool in the hands of a great craftsman can produce magnificent work.

These days I spend a lot of time reflecting on God's vocabulary, and I've concluded that what the world considers to be great things might not be all that great after all.

"When someone invites you to a wedding feast, do not sit down in the best place. It could happen that someone more important than you has been invited, and your host, who invited both of you, would have to come and say to you, 'Let him have this place.' Then you would be embarrassed and have to sit in the lowest place. Instead, when you are invited, go and sit in the lowest place, so that your host will come to you and say, 'Come on up, my friend, to a better place.' . . . For those who make themselves great will be humbled, and those who humble themselves will be made great."

Luke 14:8–11 TEV

12

the filter

Regular readers of my column know that I have a great love for coffee. I generally drink mine hot and black, but I'm not adverse to cappuccino, espresso, café au lait, or iced coffee. The one thing I do not like in my coffee, however, is coffee grounds. Nothing is more irritating than taking a sip of that silky black beverage and finding some bitter grounds tickling the back of your throat. Thank God for coffee filters.

This morning while I was picking up my first cup, I got to thinking about a different kind of filter. The day we are born, you and I begin to use and customize our image filters. The longer we live, and the more situations we encounter, the more individualized our filters become.

A person's experiences either strengthen or destroy the filter through which they view the world. Difficulties wear holes in its fabric. Positive experiences fortify our filters and help us to restrain hurtful words and actions.

Why do we need filters at all? Why doesn't God just eliminate the hard times . . . the coffee grounds in our lives? I've heard believer and unbeliever alike ask why God allows bad things to happen to good people. If you think in terms of a good cup of coffee, it is easier to understand.

The best coffee is made from good, strong, finely ground coffee beans. You may not want to drink the grounds, but you can't make a cup of coffee without them. That is why we need filters.

Most of us would not choose a filter full of holes to make our morning pot of coffee, but not every person is ready to admit he or she shouldn't have a hole-filled image filter. Holes in our human filter can send anger, hatred, frustration, self-righteousness, depression, and bitterness pouring into our lives. It can make our doctrinal positions unbearably rigid and our personalities ugly and unforgiving. When we regularly consume the unpleasant grounds of alcoholism, divorce, sickness, or other trauma, we are left with a bitter taste in our mouths. If only we would check our filters for holes!

The truth is, we all have at least a few holes in our filter. We live in a rough world—holes happen. But the longer we allow them to exist, and the bigger we allow them to become, the more we grow accustomed to the grounds at the bottom of our cups.

Some people justify their bitter coffee, saying, "I didn't make those holes in the filter." Others insist that they have the right to drink their brew any way they like. True, our circumstances made the holes, but our filters can be replaced. People may also drink whatever they choose, but God offers them something much better than grounds-filled coffee.

In Matthew 11, Jesus tells us to give him our burdens and take up his burden instead. Ours are so heavy but his burden is light. You can leave your anger, your bitterness, and all your pain with him and take a load that is much easier to carry. God will replace our filters *if* we let him. I don't know about you, but I think I'll take my coffee without the grounds, thank you.

"Come unto me, all ye that labour and are heavy laden, and I will give you rest. Take my yoke upon you, and learn of me; for I am meek and lowly in heart: and ye shall find rest unto your souls. For my yoke is easy, and my burden is light."

Matthew 11:28–30 KJV

13

aromas

My eyes remained closed, and my rebellious body deliberately snuggled deeper under the bed quilt. I wanted to shut out the harsh morning light, but at the same moment I found my senses slowly drawn toward a gentle and wonderfully familiar scent.

With sleep still tugging at my eyelids, I pulled myself upright. *Is there a reason I am leaving the warm cocoon of my bed?*

Inhaling deeply, I sighed. Ah, yes! Coffee.

On weekend mornings my dear husband rises early. Long before I wake, he brews up my morning elixir. When the scent of coffee drifts to me, I can't help but smile in my sleep.

How many times have you been blessed by the scent of something wonderful? When I was a child I remember arriving home from school to the enticing fragrance of home baked cookies. Although the thought of my mom's delicious cookies was reason enough to rejoice, what made that aroma all the more appealing was knowing that my mom wasn't making those cookies for herself or for the neighbors. She was making those cookies for her children. I can still see my mother's aproned figure as I entered the kitchen. With a big smile firmly in place, she would stretch out her hand and offer me an ever so beautifully formed, still warm from the oven, butter cookie.

Another scent always brings back wonderful memories — the bouquet of lilacs. When I was a child we had a number of lilac bushes around the home that my parents and grandparents shared. The flowers' many hues ran from deepest violet to palest lavender. The colors were beautiful, but their fragrance brings warm and comfortable memories of my grandmother flooding over me. With the slightest whiff of their perfume, I'm transported back to her cozy living room, and the touch of her hand. Her home was a wonderful sanctuary, and I will forever associate lilacs with feelings of contentment. My husband's offering of coffee on a weekend morning provides me with the same secure feeling that someone cares about me.

God is not immune to the blessing of an aromatic scent. When we pray according to his will, he receives our words as fragrant incense floating up to heaven for his pleasure. I would imagine that he gets a few unpleasant scents from us as well. Have you ever had the displeasure of interacting with some foul smell? An up-close-and-personal encounter with a skunk perhaps? Or the aggravation of having to clean up the mess left by an overturned garbage can on a hot summer's day? I imagine our grumbling and whining prayers might affect our Father in heaven the way these smells affect us.

We often turn up our noses and quickly make an exit from situations where offensive smells are present, but God does not turn away from us. No matter how objectionable our scent, he holds his arms open to embrace us. Let us pray that the fragrance of our prayers is the most sweet-scented offering we can bring to our heavenly Father.

Let my prayer be counted as [fragrant] incense before thee, and the lifting up of my hands as an evening sacrifice!

Psalm 141:2 RSV

14

instant versus brewed

W hat happened?" I squinted at my friend who sat in the blackness across from me at our favorite diner.

"The lights went out," she responded with a calm logic that only she can deliver.

"Obviously," I replied, unable to keep a touch of sarcasm out of my voice. "I was wondering why!"

The waitress arrived at that moment with a candle and a smile almost as bright. "Here you go," she said, setting the light down between us. "Apparently a transformer blew out and it will be a while before we have our electricity back. Fortunately, our ovens and grill are gas, so we'll be able to continue to serve up whatever you would like."

"I'll have a black coffee and a western omelet." I gave my order as she took out her pad.

Her smile faded. "The omelet won't be a problem, but the coffeepots are electric, so that may be more difficult. We can serve you instant though," she offered, her smile returning.

I gulped, then squeaked out a weak "okay."

Even by means of the dim candlelight I could see the grin on my friend's face. She knew what instant coffee meant to me. Given the choice of instant coffee or a bad case of the flu, I would most likely choose the flu.

Fast-food dinners, on-the-spot satellite communications, instant coffee . . . our society waits for nothing today. We want what we want, and we want it *now!* No stews left simmering on the back burner of the stove, no long letters to read on the front porch and reread later by the firelight . . . and no smell of coffee brewing deep and black, drawing everyone to the warmth of the kitchen for a late-night chat.

True, many modern conveniences save precious time, but I wonder what we forfeit in exchange. I cannot count how many momentous, reflective, and even entertaining conversations I've had with my three boys while waiting for a second pot of coffee to brew. Nor can I count the number of times I've sat up with the warmth of a freshly brewed coffee to contemplate a difficult verse of Scripture.

Coffee and contemplation seem to go well together. As the coffee trickles into the pot, I pour my prayers onto the questions that lay heavy on my heart. Soon the pot is full and so is my heart. I don't mind that the answers I seek might not come. Contemplating the questions and spending time with my Lord is enough. He holds my hand and chats with me, giving me warm comfort in my cup all the while.

Yes, it takes time to brew a good cup of coffee, but it is worth the wait.

Let us not lose heart in doing good, for in due time we will reap if we do not grow weary.

Galatians 6:9 NASB

15

meteors

I moved a bit closer to my husband for warmth and found his arm slipping comfortably around my shoulder. It happily cushioned my neck as I leaned my head still farther back to gaze at the night sky. My baby blue pajamas and slippered feet peeked merrily out from under the long, black, winter coat I donned before leaving my cozy house. At least my husband had the decency to get dressed before our stargaze, but in my sleepy state I was barely able to pull my coat on properly. Staring at the sky, my whole family was now fully awake. We'd entered the exciting world of a midnight meteor shower and were watching excitedly as God gloriously displayed his shooting stars.

"Oh, look at that one!" I began bouncing up and down as I pointed out a particularly bright meteor. "And there! There's another one." My voice was low and still a bit hoarse with the night's chill, but the whisper seemed to echo through our neighborhood like a dynamite blast.

"I see them," my husband responded in his usual under-stated manner. Yet I could see the light of the stars reflecting brightly in his eyes. They seemed to twinkle like those of a cartoon character who just kissed the pretty girl.

"Wow. This is so cool," my sixteen-year-old son, Timothy, said with obvious awe.

"Did you see that one?" his older brother, Alan, asked excitedly.

One after another the "shooting stars" streaked across the sky, accompanied by the oohs and aahs of the DuMont household. I knew these meteors were just chunks of rock and ice being destroyed in the earth's atmosphere, even as we watched their glorious demise. Yet that did not seem to matter. Their fiery beauty held us captive.

Then, during one of our few moments of silence, I heard the chattering of other families down the street. In the stillness of the night air, their voices carried to us as clear as children shouting to each other through opposite ends of a drainpipe. To my great surprise, I found that this sky-filled performance was not a private show! They were laughing and commenting on the wonders of the evening display just as we were.

God provided a pageant in the heavens for all of his creation to enjoy. It did not matter that some attending the show were not personally acquainted with the Creator and Director of the performance. For the moment at least, none could or would deny his existence, and he was more than happy to share the magnificence of the heavens with all of us.

I returned to my bed within the hour, but my mind was no longer eager to catch the sleep my body still craved. An extra cup of coffee in the morning might be necessary to get me moving, but for now I wanted to revel in the grandeur and awe of God that filled my soul. My limited understanding had been opened to snatches of God's character. His splendor, majesty, and greatness was only minutely reflected in the shooting stars I saw — but I'd been given a glimpse of heaven, his home. . . .

Look up into the heavens. Who created all the stars? He brings them out one after another, calling each by its name. And he counts them to see that none are lost or have strayed away.

Isaiah 40:26 NLT

16

choir rehearsal

The angelic music of Christmas surrounds me tonight. Our church choir is rehearsing for their annual candlelight Christmas concert. While they weave their glorious music through the air, my laptop is busy taking down these words. I am not a member of the choir . . . and for good reason. Not only can't I read music, but I can't sing a single note on key. Those with the gift of music, like my husband and my children, must cringe when I, with great abandon, sing the Sunday hymns. But God does not require us to sing beautifully; he simply requires us to rejoice with him and use the gifts he has given us.

As I sip my coffee and tap the keyboard, I can't help but wish that my vocal cords would cooperate with my deep desire to praise his name in song. Instead, I choose each word I write carefully and attempt to express my joy and appreciation for the nature of my God in prose. As I write, my mind reels with countless questions. Does God sing? Does he write? What *is* God like?

One aspect of God is clear in my mind—he is a creative being. He demonstrated that when he created everything from grand galaxies to minute microbes. The Bible says he created humans in his image. If this is true, it stands to reason that we too should be creative. Of course we are not perfect the way God is perfect. God embodies every creative ability there is. Even the Michelangelos of this world can only boast an insignificant portion of that.

Some people were given the ability to create exquisite music, some grand sculptures, and still others great works of literature. My youngest sister has the talent of creating the most beautiful items out of absolutely nothing. Finding an old dresser, she turned it into a work of art with nothing more than a paintbrush and her vivid imagination. When she touches a piece of paper, complex, multifaceted stars emerge, and at her touch gorgeous fall wreaths materialize from a bunch of dried-up twigs. My older sister is a baker and pastry chef. She creates magnificent wedding cakes that are almost too beautiful to eat. My father spent years creatively fixing machinery of all sorts and now spends his retirement carving beautiful art out of pieces of discarded wood. Last but certainly not least is my mom. Her hands are never idle. She crochets and weaves a wonderful assortment of gifts for everyone she meets.

But creativity is not limited to the arts. I recently talked to a woman who told me she was not the least creative. Yet when I observed her working with a group of young children, she found the most innovative ways of capturing their attention. Even the very coffee I drink is grown by a person with the ability to nurture plants, and it is sold by another's ingenious aptitude to market a product. God has given us all talent and ability. How we choose to use his gifts is up to us.

As each one has received a special gift, employ it in serving one another as good stewards of the manifold grace of God.

1 Peter 4:10 NASB

46

nutmeg hope

I wrapped my hands around a large paper coffee cup and allowed its warmth to seep through the liner and deep into my cold fingers. Even with the car running and the heater blasting, December's frigid air chilled me to the bone. On this freezing morning I'd decided to treat myself to a hot latte at the local coffee shop before work. For a moment I was content to simply soak up the bit of warmth afforded me by holding my cup, but in short order the smell of nutmeg drew my eyes down to the cup's contents.

A fluff of foamy cream sat on top of the beverage, and sprinkled ever so delicately upon this cloud was freshly grated nutmeg. Its scent mingled with that of the coffee and cream, and I sighed with contentment as this reminder of the upcoming holidays saturated my brain as well as my nostrils. This was the smell of hope.

Nutmeg and Christmas are as bound together in my mind as the red and white stripes on a candy cane. One leads inevitably to the other, each complementing and enhancing the holiday. Christmas is also my season of hope. As a child, there was of course the hope that I would receive the one special gift I craved. During my teen years and the Vietnam crisis, an idealistic thread of hope for world peace remained firmly entrenched in my soul. When I grew into a woman, I embraced the magical hope of romantic love and the future that lay ahead. But these were only shadows of something deeper—a hope and peace that goes beyond human understanding.

Hope was meant to be the nutmeg on top of the coffee. It is what draws an individual toward the real substance. A person would not consider eating a heaping spoonful of grated nutmeg. The unpleasant aftertaste would defer any ideas of repeating the process. Hope for its own sake can be empty and taste bitter. Something of substance must lie underneath, something on which the hope stands.

Hope misplaced will also fall short of our expectations. Imagine nutmeg sprinkled on a crisp dill pickle! Hope must be correctly placed. It takes a savvy individual to realize that hoping for good health, a home full of perfect children, and all the material goods in the world won't plug the ache at the core of a person's soul.

A sprinkling of nutmeg on top of the cream truly enhances the coffee's flavor, but without the coffee . . . the nutmeg is nothing. Hope by itself is nothing. Hope misplaced is nothing. Christ is where hope should direct us. If we allow our hope for a future to lead us to an eternity with Christ, then our hope was well placed.

May your next Christmas be filled with *the* hope that will truly fill your spirit and the season with joy beyond measure.

And his name will be the hope of all the world.

Matthew 12:21 NLT

18

spilled coffee

I gripped my steaming cup of coffee as if holding it tighter would somehow keep me from spilling the contents onto my cream-colored turtleneck and new khaki trousers. The blackness that filled the room was a pure contrast to the bright fluorescent lighting of a few moments before. A power failure of some sort left me in an uncomfortable situation. I was seated in a church classroom, in one of those grade-school chairs with the desk attached to one arm. For a child to slip in and out of such a seat is usually not a problem. For a not-so-agile, middle-aged woman with a very full cup of scalding hot coffee to arise from this same chair in the dark, well that is quite another matter.

Over the sound of thunder and rain, I heard uneasy laughter as a woman in our church kitchen called out that she could not find a flashlight. Down the hall two men talked in serious tones as they fumbled and bumped their way toward the electrical circuit box. I assumed they would soon flip the correct switch and restore normalcy. These people were trying to find a cure for the problem. As one drop of very hot coffee found its way down the side of the cup onto my bare hand, their efforts seemed even more admirable.

Then I heard it. Drifting in my direction were exquisite strains of joyous praise. Compelled to discover the source of the sound, I decided to take a risk. Ever so slowly I moved the hot coffee toward the side of my chair, away from any certain personal damage, and then set it on the floor next to me. Once I accomplished this grand feat, I allowed the sweet melody to lead me around the remaining desks and toward the choir room.

Goose bumps ran the length of my arms as I approached the door. The room's blackness was filled with the musical strains of a soloist. Her lovely soprano lifted praises to God with no concern for the darkness at all. It was as if the piano music was God's voice. It said, "Just listen to me. Don't look around and don't concern yourself with what you can or cannot see. I am your reality. Concentrate on me."

The notes rang deep and sincere. The music played. The soloist sang.

When the lights came on, I quietly slipped back to the other room. My coffee remained right where I'd set it. Not a drop had spilled. Why was I so worried? It was just coffee.

The woman who sought the flashlight came into the room and we chatted for a moment. Gone was her nervous laughter. The two men who diligently searched for the breaker box returned as well. Gone were their serious tones. They joked lightheartedly about the return of the lights. Apparently, they came on just as the men had arrived at the box.

The situation reminded me of how I often handle the little blackouts in my own life. I am a fixer by nature, and my tendency is to jump right in and look for a solution to every difficulty. The problem is that searching for a solution isn't always what God wants me to do. Maybe all God wants me to do is pay closer attention to the music.

I know, O LORD, that the way of human beings is not in their control, that mortals as they walk cannot direct their steps.

Jeremiah 10:23

50

19

cherry beans
and dancing goats

I recently came across an interesting tidbit of coffee history. It seems that around A.D. 850, a goatherder named Kaldi lived a peaceful life in the mountains of what is now known as Ethiopia. One evening when his goats did not return home as they usually did, he took up his staff and set out to look for them. To his great alarm he found the usually calm and compliant flock dancing and frolicking like young kids high up the mountainside. *What would make them act like this?* he wondered.

Concerned that his flock might be the target of some demonic trickery, he did not approach them immediately but watched for a short time from a nearby ridge. Before long he believed he knew the true reason for the goats' behavior. They were feasting on some unknown red berries. Despite the fact that he did not recognize this shiny-leafed shrub, he decided to sample the fruit himself to be sure his theory was correct. The surge of energy that came upon him when he chewed the berries made him realize that this was indeed a special plant. He hurried into town bringing along a parcel of the fruit, and the rest is history. Over a third of the world's population now consumes coffee—the leading countries being the good old U.S.A. and Germany. As an American of German heritage, it should come as no surprise that I love my coffee.

What did surprise me was that my beloved beverage comes not from a bean but from a fruit seed! Technically it comes from a cherry. The coffee "bean" is one of two seeds inside each piece of fruit. Never would I have guessed that those fragrant, brown, toasted nuggets that pour into my little coffee grinder each weekend morning are cherry pits! Things are not always what they appear to be.

God often asks us to look beyond our circumstances to see his larger plan. He asks us to believe the unbelievable and to see what others cannot. God asked Abraham and Sarah to believe that two senior citizens could conceive a child and produce a great nation (Genesis 18). Noah was asked to believe that God would destroy the whole earth and that he would save humanity by loading one family into a huge ship built on dry land. He was six hundred years old when all this finally took place (Genesis 6–8). An insignificant beggar was asked to believe that spit placed on his eyes would help restore his sight (Mark 8:23), and two sisters were asked to look beyond their brother's grave, to new life (John 11).

Individuals today are asked to believe that broken marriages can be restored and that a child whose innocence has been taken can be healed. They are also asked to believe that God came down to earth to live with man and that his name was Jesus. All of these requests ask humans to look beyond our circumstances and beyond what seems possible. I'm glad that the One True God of heaven and earth is still the God of miracles. I may never see the waters of the Jordan parted to make a dry path for my afternoon walk, but I still believe in God's ability to do the impossible.

Be not forgetful to entertain strangers: for thereby some have entertained angels unawares.

Hebrews 13:2 KJV

20

hope continuously

My coffee this morning has a decidedly bitter taste. I've noticed that tears mixed with coffee tend to unpleasantly turn its taste. As I talk on the phone with my mom, we discuss the cancer that was discovered in my dad only a few weeks ago. It is the first day of a new year, and the future that only a few weeks ago seemed secure, now appears unsure.

In talking to my mom, I express my concern about the surgery that will take place in mid-January. My father's cancerous organs must be removed. Dad's not a young man, and the operation alone will take its toll on him. We don't know where else the cancer may have spread, and that worries me as well. I share these thoughts with my mom, not to add to her concerns but to assure myself that she understands the risk . . . and all of its possibilities. From both her tears and her words I know she grasps the seriousness of it all. Then a strange thing happens. She laughs. She says we have no reason to worry yet. The possibility still exists that the doctor can remove all the cancer. Mom talks about woodworking projects that Dad intends to start this year. She acknowledges that he is often too tired to work on anything now, but she hopes that his strength will return. The change in her voice is dramatic.

Does she understand that my dad, her husband of over fifty years, may die? I ask her quietly if she is okay and again mention that the cancer might take Dad's life. At first she is quiet and then she responds with a strength that I know comes from her faith in Christ. She tells me that she fully understands, but until that day comes, she will continue to hope for his recovery. I no longer hear tears in her voice but something else. Trust perhaps?

We laugh about some small matters and share details about the snowstorm that covers the northern part of the country. My mother's own health is not good, and a serious tone again creeps into my voice as I ask how she is feeling. In the past such a question might have brought on a review of various aches that plague seniors her age, but this time it did not. She simply says that she is doing well . . . all things considered.

Our conversation ends on a cheerful note. As I hang up the phone I can't quite let go of our little talk. Hope surges in me like a fountain springing from the desert. My hope has been seeded by hers. I know that God is sovereign and that he may take my dad to be with him at any time, but I also know that God calls us to think on things that are good, noble, praiseworthy, lovely, and of good report (Phil. 4:8). He calls us to hope for the best, and I, like my mother, will not give up hope.

When I am called to leave this earth, I trust that I will accept those circumstances with equal graciousness. I pray that I never become so earthbound as to give up the hope that God can, and just might, touch our lives in some special way. I know that God will provide mercy and grace to deal with the reality we all must endure. Both life and death can be difficult, but I choose to hope for the best and praise his goodness to the end.

But I will hope continually, and will praise thee yet more and more.

Psalm 71:14 ASV

grow where you
are planted

All coffee is grown within a thousand miles of the equator, from the Tropic of Cancer in the north to the Tropic of Capricorn in the south. A thousand miles may seem like quite a bit of property, but in the scheme of the universe, it is only a very thin band around the center of our earth. Anyone investing in a coffee plantation north or south of these boundaries is asking for trouble. God positions his coffee plants in an environment perfect for their success. We humans might prefer to live in our air-conditioned, dehumidified environments, but for the coffee plant, the equator is pretty close to heaven.

Obviously not all plants thrive under the same conditions. A beautiful flowering bush grew in our yard when I was a girl. As I prepared to mow our lawn each summer, my father would say, "Don't forget to run into the bush!" Some people might think that sort of reminder to be just a little crazy. Why would my father *want* us to damage his precious foliage? Finally I asked him. "Because that bush only blooms where it is bruised," he answered.

Some people thrive and grow under adversity. They seek out the fellowship and advice of other believers more often when pressures take their toll. They are on their knees earlier in the morning and later at night, and find themselves in God's presence at the oddest moments of the day when misfortune enters their lives. When life becomes difficult, God can make some people more, not less, compassionate, giving, caring, and useful.

Some people spend half their lives complaining about their jobs, their families, and their living situations. Others have learned that where we are and the situations we encounter are God ordained. Like the coffee plant, God sets people in the best locations for their development. He waters them with as much or as little rain as needed for the personality of each individual. If your personality is like that of a cactus, God might allow you to store up the life-giving waters needed to get you through some dry times. If you respond to God like a delicate fern, perhaps God will shade you from the intensity of evil influences. If you resemble a coffee plant, perhaps your fruit will need to be cracked, roasted, and ground for others to taste the wealth that God supplied for you.

I think it best to spend my time flourishing in the soil where God planted me instead of trying to uproot myself to some seemingly lovely but less-suitable environment. The grass may be greener on the other side of the fence, but that may not be the best place for me to grow.

Not that I speak in regard to need, for I have learned in whatever state I am, to be content: I know how to be abased, and I know how to abound. Everywhere and in all things I have learned both to be full and to be hungry, both to abound and to suffer need.

Philippians 4:11–12 NKJV

22

the foolishness of God

Life reminds me a lot of a jigsaw puzzle . . . and I love jig-saw puzzles almost as much as I love coffee. When you first take a puzzle out of its box, you find yourself staring at hundreds of little misshapen bits of cardboard. Each fragment contains a seemingly irrelevant concoction of colors and shapes. The task before you is daunting. Should you start with daz-zling crimson pieces or those with the mottled blue specks?

Jigsaw enthusiasts, like myself, usually start with the "edge" pieces. We pick through the box bit by bit and set apart any piece that has a straight side. Then we sort those possible side pieces into color categories and begin to determine which belong together. Eventually the border takes shape, and with it, an idea of where the colors and patterns begin and end.

I think God wants to build our lives this way. When we are young all we see are disconnected pieces. Upon meeting my husband for the first time, I knew that he was the most won-derful boy I'd ever met. He was funny, smart, handsome, ath-letic, and to my sheer delight, he was a musician in a rock band. He was headed toward college, I toward the world of work.

These were the first elements of our puzzle. They reflected a wondrous array of colors, shapes, and patterns, but I had no idea how they would fit together in the grand scheme of my life. After high school John and I became more serious about our relationship. The border of our lives began to form and patterns emerged. Still, it was many years later before enough pieces were in place to allow images to surface. The images were based on things my husband and I put into our lives — bits of the puzzle we put together. A number of very bright pieces fell into place as we married, as we had our three sons, and as I rededicated my life to Christ. Fifteen years into our marriage another brilliant section emerged as my husband also gave his life to Jesus and began serving Christ. Millions of small events filled the space in between. Some of the pieces were difficult to place. I knew they were a part of our puzzle; I just could not seem to fit them in at first. There were dark pieces that I wished I could ignore, but they were a part of the puzzle too. Without them I could not connect the bright pieces. When I finally inserted those sinister fragments, I stepped back to look at the picture that was forming. Oddly the colorful sections were all the more obvious now that they lay next to the dark ones.

The more pieces I connect to our puzzle, the more I realize that God has an incredible plan for our lives. He gives us each the pieces we need, but it is up to us to put them together. When we refuse to accept parts we don't like or look for pieces that should not be a part of our puzzle, we can't finish the beautiful picture God has planned.

My coffee cup is almost empty as I put the last piece of my Christmas puzzle in its place. My life puzzle still has a lot of missing pieces. As I get older, it gets easier to see where things fit, and I'm less reluctant to put in the dark pieces. God is good and I know he has a wonderful plan.

Because the foolishness of God is wiser than men, and the weakness of God is stronger than men.

1 Corinthians 1:25 NKJV

23

shopping around

People have very different ideas about where they can get the best cup of coffee.

Convenience Coffee

Some coffee lovers choose the convenience of purchasing their morning brew at the local doughnut or bagel shop. Most of these folks enjoy coffee but are not die-hard fans. They want their coffee quick and with no frills.

I've noticed some no-frills churchgoers too. They don't care where they worship so long as the service is short and they can get back home in a reasonable amount of time. Don't ask them to come early for Sunday school, attend a midweek committee meeting, or stay after the service for fellowship. They want to get in and get out. Just as convenience coffee drinkers often miss out on relationships formed over a cup of coffee, I've found that many "convenience Christians" miss one excellent part of the Christian experience—fellowship with other believers.

Mall Coffee

Some coffee lovers like the trendy mall establishments, which serve gourmet coffees in every imaginable flavor and style. You can get your coffee hot, iced, whip-creamed, spiced, black, brown, or even green on St. Patrick's Day.

Some Christians prefer to attend churches with lots of variety and an assortment of programs. They want choices for every stage of life, every imaginable activity, and every time of day. "I don't want to get bored" is their motto.

Ambiance and Coffee

Ambiance is the key ingredient for the socially astute coffee drinker. He or she cares less for the coffee than its presentation. These types usually head for the more elite coffeehouses that cater to the refined taste.

Churchgoers in the ambiance category are the first to check out the stained glass windows, the altar coverings, and whether the flowers in the sanctuary are fresh and fragrant. Pews should be padded, the organ perfectly tuned, and the preaching concerned with only the most politically correct, contemporary issues. None of this is negotiable.

Coffee as an Accompaniment

Dessert fans know that nothing goes with a slice of cheesecake or a dish of chocolate ice cream like a good cup of coffee. Iced tea and ice cream or root beer and cheesecake just won't do.

Some churchgoers feel that a worship service goes nicely with an Easter sunrise and Christmas Eve candlelight. They joyously attend these services as an accompaniment to the other festivities of the season but certainly don't want to partake of church on a regular basis.

Everyday Refreshment

Of course, many of us start off every morning with a fine cup of coffee and then refresh ourselves with a late afternoon one as well. For us, coffee goes with everything, so having it with our breakfast bagel or lunchtime lunch meat is just as good as having it with dessert.

Some of us think that God goes well with everything too. We bless the food he provides at meals, spend time in the Scriptures before the day begins, and end each evening chatting with our heavenly Father.

How do you like your coffee?

"Keep these words that I am commanding you today in your heart. Recite them to your children and talk about them when you are at home and when you are away, when you lie down and when you rise."

Deuteronomy 6:6–7

24

coffee for gold

A young man clutched in his fist a great wad of worthless bills. His attempt to purchase a flint for his lighter had failed. Apparently the cost of a new flint had risen since he'd returned from the war. A flint was now worth one precious chicken egg, far more than he owned. "Goods for goods" was the policy of the day. The paper money he'd been given for his army service was not even worth the cost of its own ink.

The young man's face remained expressionless as he watched a much older gentleman goad a wheelbarrow down the cavity-riddled street in front of him. The conveyance was filled with the same paper money the young man still pitifully gripped in his own hand. As the elderly man turned toward the once-thriving bakery in attempt to purchase a loaf of bread with his mountain of useless cash, the younger man forced himself to turn away. He knew the outcome of the exchange that would take place and could only shake his head. Slowly, he relaxed his grip on the useless paper and watched it float onto the street like the garbage it was.

In a nearby town a young kindergarten teacher and her mother discussed the girl's upcoming wedding. Her mother, a seamstress, had, despite the hard times, managed to eke out a living sewing for some of the wealthier townspeople. The girl's father had been absent since long before the war.

When war broke out between the United States and Germany, the girl's father, who had left to find work in America, was forced to put the reunion of his family on hold. Now the war was over. Her mother would soon join her father overseas . . . but first there would be a wedding. Her mother's loving hands had sewed the gown, field flowers would adorn her bouquet, and wild rabbit would be served at the feast. There was one item, however, they could not seem to manage — the wedding bands. Then the package arrived.

The girl's father sent canned meat to supplement the wedding feast. He also found a way to supply nylon stockings, cigarettes, and the most precious item of all — American coffee. The bride's tears flowed freely. If one could buy such luxuries in America, there was hope. But now was not the time to dawdle. The gifts from America needed to be traded for gold that could be fashioned into two wedding bands.

This story is not fiction. My parents' wedding bands were actually purchased in post–World War II Germany with coffee sent from America by my grandfather. As amazing as it may seem, God used my favorite beverage to purchase the symbol of their faithfulness to each other.

I love to hear my dad and mom recount this story and others, even though some of the circumstances they describe are difficult for me to imagine. Perhaps living through such trials helped develop the faith that now comes so easily to them. They in truth know the power of Almighty God. They do not look for miracles at every turn, yet they do not waver in their belief that God can and does perform miracles even today. My parents' belief that God provides for each person's needs is unshakable.

Like my dad says, "God gives me what I need. If I don't have something, then I didn't need it in the first place." Amen, Dad.

"If you then, being evil, know how to give good gifts to your children, how much more will your Father who is in heaven give good things to those who ask Him!"

Matthew 7:11 NKJV

25

caffeine kick

Two of my kids were just getting over painful ear infections, the Christmas holidays were fast approaching, and I coveted Sleeping Beauty's endless night more than all the gold in Fort Knox. The day ahead of me did not have a catnap in sight. Maybe one more cup of coffee would help me through.

As I poured the last of that morning's pot into my mug, I could not help but wonder why the first four mugs were not having more influence on my body's sleepy state. It used to take only one cup to get me into the swing of the morning. Lately I'd been pouring more and more java to get myself moving.

The above scenario occurred over fifteen years ago . . . before I set my three-cup-per-day limit. When I found my caffeine needs getting out of hand, I did a little research. Caffeine is not addictive but it certainly is habit forming. Here is what I discovered.

Despite what most people believe, caffeine does not actually give you more vigor, it simply fools your body into thinking it isn't tired. When fatigue settles into your limbs after a long day, your brain produces a chemical called adenosine. This chemical travels to receptor cells where it stops other chemicals from stimulating your brain. Without their prompting, you feel weary and your body is forced to rest.

Caffeine mimics adenosine by closing up the receptor cells. Your body thinks the adenosine has filled the cells and that it is doing its job, but it's not. Your brain never gets the signal to slow down, so you feel more awake. But God knows that our bodies need rest, so he made our bodies smarter than the caffeine in order to foil its tricks. When a person's brain figures out that the body needs rest, it makes additional receptor cells. When this happens, your usual amount of caffeine can't keep you awake.

Now comes an even bigger problem. Your body made way too many receptor cells and it *needs* large doses of caffeine to plug up those extra cells. You've created a habit that forces you to drink more and more caffeinated beverages. It only takes a week for this to happen. If you take the cold-turkey route to kick the habit, your body will need two weeks to reduce the number of receptor cells to a normal level. Headaches, lethargy, fatigue, and muscle pain are the price you will pay for your coffee obsession.

Caffeine in moderation is a wonderful thing. It helps a person adhere to a task. Driving the kids home from their long weekend youth retreat or staying up until your teen gets home from his first night out with your new car is just a bit easier with a cup of hot coffee. The key is restraint. Ice cream is delicious, but you can't live without your veggies. Most of my beverage consumption is unadulterated tap water now, but somehow that makes the selected few cups of coffee I allow myself all the more special.

He who neglects discipline despises himself, but he who listens to reproof acquires understanding.

Proverbs 15:32 NASB

26

two men

The sun set behind the picturesque white church building where two men stood in deep conversation. The older man was impeccably dressed. His expensive charcoal gray suit was finished off with a deep blue shirt, a silk gray tie, and highly polished shoes. The younger man, although neat and clean, sported only a pair of faded jeans and pullover fleece jacket. His running shoes were well worn and untied.

From where I sat sipping my coffee on a nearby bench, I could not overhear the conversation, but their animated expressions proved that each was trying to convince the other of something. For a long time the conversation was passionate but not heated. Then the tide turned. In a sudden burst of anger, the older man reached into his pocket then flung its contents onto the pavement. With fury in his eyes, he turned toward his car. The younger man called after him but there was no response. After the elder gentleman drove away, I could see tears in the eyes of the remaining man. He picked up the discarded paper and held it for just a moment, then quietly walked to a brimming trash can that stood on the street corner and sadly dropped the paper onto the heap. Having done this, he walked toward the church, opening the door as strains of music wafted through the air.

I was undeniably curious as to what had provoked this argument. Like a detective on a hot lead, I glanced around to see if anyone else was watching. The trash can held my clue. I walked over to it and set down my half-full cup of coffee while gingerly retrieving the discarded paper from among the cast-off fast-food wrappings and dirty soda cans. It was a ticket . . . and not just any ticket, mind you. It was a box seat ticket to the World Series game being played that night.

I tossed the squandered ticket back onto the trash and slowly made my way up the church steps. I just had to know. What was so important that this young man was willing to give up such a precious ticket? Inside the church the music continued to play softly. I was surprised to find the church nearly empty. Only a few men and women gathered around the front altar. I crept forward and listened as the prayers grew louder.

"Father, we come before you tonight to dedicate this child in the presence of your people," the white-haired minister pronounced as he held a cooing child in his arms. The group of men and women gathered with him each took a turn laying a hand on the babe's head while they prayed for the child. The young man who'd been outside arguing with the older gentleman now stood slightly to the side of the group, his arm protectively around a delicate young woman who was obviously the child's mother. Both fairly beamed as blessings were bestowed on the child. When the dedication was complete, the young mother carefully took the child into her own waiting arms as the father encircled them both, shedding tears mixed with joy and sorrow.

Now I understood. This man had forsaken the temptation of his earthly father in order to dedicate his newborn son to his heavenly Father. I don't know why God allowed these circumstances, but I do know that in the end joy won.

Make me understand the way of thy precepts, and I will meditate on thy wondrous works.

Psalm 119:27 RSV

27

kaffe zeit

L uisa, *Kaffe Zeit!*" At times I can still hear my mother calling me, despite the eight-hundred-plus miles between us. If only I could oblige her!

Although *Kaffe Zeit* means "coffee time" in my native German tongue, this afternoon breather consists of so much more than simply drinking coffee. Sweets are usually served along with the coffee. Rich whipped cream tortes, fruit-laden tarts, and melt-in-your-mouth butter cookies were only a few of the possible offerings if company joined us. My mom seldom had to call me twice. Along with my love for coffee, I have a real weakness for desserts.

Our daily *Kaffe Zeit* became a thing of the past when my family came to the United States. The time-honored German custom of leisurely breaking for coffee each afternoon was set aside for the American tradition of grabbing a quick cup and returning to work . . . except on Sunday. Then my mom tuned out the world, put on the coffeepot, and brought out the home-baked goods. There is something extra special about coffee served with cake or cookies. The slight bite of this beverage is the perfect match for the sweet creaminess of cheesecake or the crisp snap of a thin wafer cookie. As a child, this wonderful blend of coffee and sweets was not lost on me. *Kaffe Zeit* was one of my favorite events. As I became older and my insight grew, I realized that the confectioneries and the tasty beverage were only a small part of the pleasure. The purpose of coffee time was to stop your work in order to delight in life's pleasures.

Germans are known for putting their shoulder to the wheel. I was raised to believe jobs should be done to the best of your ability. There was no shame in work done well, and no job was beneath a good worker. After a week of labor, the pleasure of coffee served in a china cup with family and friends in pleasant conversation was a treat in and of itself.

But the most important part of coffee time was that we were *required* to take this break. We took it off with no guilt and no hesitation. This was time to be savored. The work would wait for us and when we returned to it, we would do so with renewed vigor. During coffee time we would sit, laugh, rest, and enjoy God's bounty.

Much can be learned from this practice. The world of the twenty-first century tells us we need to rush around 24/7, but God specifically calls us to take a break. At coffee time we sip our coffee, a staple in German homes, and we are reminded that God supplies our everyday needs. We nibble our special treats and realize that he also supplies special blessings that we did not ask for. We laugh with our family and friends and want to thank him not only for our lives, but for the lives of those who share a relationship with us. I'm grateful that my mother taught me to work hard, but I'm also glad she reminded me to take a break with the one who provides me with the ability to do so.

For in six days the Lord made the heavens and the earth, the sea, and all that is in them, and rested the seventh day. Therefore the Lord blessed the Sabbath day and hallowed it.

Exodus 20:11 NKJV

28

pots

I could not restrain a sigh as I viewed the large assortment of coffeepots available in the specialty store. I was looking for something out of the ordinary for a fellow coffee lover who was getting married, but until I entered this store I had no idea how difficult my choice would be. A salesperson approached me and cleverly asked, "Can I help you?"

"Yes, I'm looking for a coffeepot," I responded almost as smartly.

"Hmm . . . what kind?"

I wanted to respond with, "If I knew that, I would not be standing here like a dunce," but I held my tongue and just shrugged my shoulders.

The salesgirl smiled at my naiveté and began to recite the attributes of the various kinds of pots.

There were electric percolators, but she confidently told me that these were stone-age technology. One did not boil the coffee bean any longer.

There was a very large assortment of drip pots, apparently the most popular kind of coffeemaker. Dozens of manufacturers vied for this market. Some of these pots were small and advertised their ability to make a quick cup without distortion of flavor. Others cost a small fortune and promoted multiple features—everything from simple warming plates with mini- and maxibrew cycles to timers that would allow you to wake up to the scent of coffee while never leaving your cozy bed. Drip coffeepots came in an array of wonderful sizes, colors, and shapes too. Some had carafes, others stout and sturdy receptacles. Each offered you the very best coffee you ever tasted.

There were of course many choices that were less ordinary. Some of these coffeemakers offered thermal carafes, mild frothers, and built-in coffee grinders. Cappuccino and espresso makers abounded, and there was even a Turkish coffeemaker that looked something like an inverted brass teacup attached to a long wooden handle. From the information on the side of its box, I got the impression that this pot was meant to be heated in the hot desert sand. It did state, however, that the top of a stove would work if the former were not available.

The salesgirl was quick to show me her personal favorite— a French coffee press. These too came in a variety of styles. The stainless steel ones offered years of reliability, and the plastic version shouted both its cost effectiveness and convenience.

What was I to do? I thanked the salesgirl and suggested she give me a few moments to reflect on the alternatives. A little miffed that I did not immediately take to her recommendation, she smiled a crooked smile and turned to what I'm sure she hoped would be a more appreciative customer.

As I wandered the aisles I noticed that there were customers for each type of pot. Some apparently did prefer the archaic electric percolator, because despite the salesclerk's disdain, one older woman took a shiny chrome one to the register. Many chose the drip pots, and a few chose the cappuccino and espresso makers. I did not see anyone buy a Turkish coffeepot, but I assured myself that the store would not stock such an item unless there was a market.

Looking at all the pots reminded me of the variety God created in his people. Some prefer the hand-clapping music of the

71

Pentecostal church, some the more traditional liturgical service of mainstream Protestant denominations, and still others may prefer a small and intimate independent Bible church. The many coffeepots I had to choose from all made some form of coffee; likewise, every church that bases its faith on the solid rock of Jesus the Messiah is a part of the beautiful body of Christ.

Now I plead with you, brethren, by the name of our Lord Jesus Christ, that you all speak the same thing, and that there be no divisions among you, but that you be perfectly joined together in the same mind and in the same judgment. For it has been declared to me . . . that there are contentions among you.

1 Corinthians 1:10–11 NKJV

29

training

I watched my friend cover the ground at our local high school track in remarkable time. Arms loose at her sides, feet firmly planted with each stride, mouth slightly open . . . she looked the picture of a good athlete. One would think she'd been doing this for years, but in truth she only began training a short time ago. Although younger than I am, she is no teenager. Undertaking this activity required more than good intentions. Her rapidly growing love for running grew into a passion that demanded a goal. She wanted to participate in a marathon. However, my savvy friend knew that even perfect form combined with passion would not be enough to win or even finish a demanding race.

The quickest start, the most rigorously kept rituals, and the most fervent love for the sport do not by themselves bring you to the finish line. Neither do the cute shorts and brightly colored tank tops that sometimes adorn less-experienced participants. My friend understands that what a marathon runner needs most is preparation and perseverance.

Just a few missed practices during the last months of training might easily set the stage for failure. Every muscle must be kept at peak performance, stretched and worked with regularity and persistence. Timing must be kept under control as well. Spending all your energy bursting from the blocks may leave an individual drained and unable to finish the race. Too slow a start and a person can fall behind. This might lead to discouragement and an overwhelming desire to quit before giving one's best effort. Practice and training help runners find the right pace.

Paul talks about our Christian life being a race of sorts where there are many runners but only one prize. I'm not sure that my friend expects to win her first marathon, but I am sure she is striving to finish it. No one starts a race anticipating that they will quit halfway, though some do find that necessary. Fatigue, torn muscles, cramps, and heat exhaustion take their toll on those participants who did not prepare well or made unwise choices.

Coffee may be a wonderful beverage, but no runner in his right mind would grab coffee from those offering a drink at the side of the road during the race. Replacing lost fluids by drinking a natural diuretic could be deadly at worst, foolish at best. You need to fill your body with fluids perfect for running a long race. Runners prepare for a race as if they are going to battle. Faulty preparation can be as fatal as putting on faulty armor.

I wonder if I am preparing properly for God's race. At times I find myself overly concerned with how my running outfit looks to others and too unconcerned with practicing my faith. When rain muddies the track, a runner may not feel like training, and when difficult circumstances muddy my path, I don't feel much like practicing my Christianity. I've noticed that not many people have registered for God's race and that a few who did sign up are getting discouraged. I wonder . . . could part of my training include working out with a friend? That might just encourage us both.

Do you not know that those who run in a race all run, but one receives the prize? Run in such a way that you may obtain it.

1 Corinthians 9:24 NKJV

30

bedroom rain

"John, wake up! It's raining in the bedroom!" I shoved my husband's shoulder, desperate to get his attention.

"Umm . . . okay," was his only sleep-laden response.

Dragging my damp sleepwear out from under the covers, I pulled my soggy feet up underneath my legs. Shaking him now, I fairly shouted, "Get *up!* I'm telling you, it's raining in the bedroom!"

Not to be disturbed by an obviously crazy wife, my now-roused husband responded with just a hint of annoyance, "It *can't* be raining in the bedroom. We are on the second floor of a three-floor house. Even if the roof were leaking, it would *not* be raining in our bedroom. Go back to sleep. You're having a bad dream.".

Okay, I thought. *Desperate circumstances call for desperate measures.* I jumped out of bed and turned our soaking wet quilt so the brunt of its soggy bulk would land squarely on the form of my once-again snoozing husband.

Now he was awake. Jumping out of bed as well, he immediately went to turn on the light.

"No! Don't turn on the electricity!" I fairly shouted. "The water is coming in through the light." I pointed at our over-head fixture. In the dim morning light filtering through the window, we could see water dripping over the edge of our ceiling fixtures.

Together we ran up to the third floor and opened the door that separated it from the rest of the house. Cold air hit us like a freezer blast. We padded barefoot to the two partly finished bedrooms and peered into each. Nothing looked amiss there. I shivered as we approached the third room, an unfinished attic. Even before we opened the door we could hear the dreadful sound of moving water. My brave husband did not even flinch; he pulled at the door. Together we watched as burst pipes showered the entire area with water, seeping through the floor into our bedroom below.

As young homeowners we'd invested our last dime to purchase this house. Zone heating allowed us to reduce costs by radically lowering the heat in our unused third floor. That cold winter night, temperatures dropped to below freezing and the pipes in the less-insulated room above our bedroom froze. The rest is history.

This year John and I celebrated our twenty-sixth wedding anniversary. Over a nice restaurant dinner and numerous cups of coffee, we reminisced, laughing about that day some twenty-two years earlier. I can honestly say that it was no laughing matter back then.

Our first home had been advertised as a handyman's delight. It didn't take long to figure out where the handyman part came in, but the *delight* part never seemed to materialize. It took every spare cent to repair the plumbing and insulate the attic that first year. The second year we had a little fire in the bathroom and decided to concentrate on the electrical work. By the third year, I'd had it with the fire-engine red carpeting throughout the house. We replaced that and got to some of the cosmetic details — like paint. Seven years passed before we were able to purchase another home. I remember our new realtor asking me what sort of house we were looking for this time. The only thing I could blurt out was that I wanted one we didn't have to fix for a while!

It was years before we could see the lessons taught us in that first house. Now on the other side of those days, I'm grateful that the Father thought us worthy to endure them.

My brethren, count it all joy when you fall into various trials, knowing that the testing of your faith produces patience. But let patience have its perfect work, that you may be perfect and complete, lacking nothing.

James 1:2–4 NKJV

31

the bitterness seed

My stomach grumbled, a reminder that my lunch hour had passed. I set aside the spreadsheet I was working on and reached my arms high above my head like a cat stretching out after a long afternoon's nap. It was definitely time to take a break. I switched off my desk light and headed toward the coffee station, eagerly anticipating the warm comfort that would accompany the cold sandwich I'd brought from home.

When I arrived at the coffee station, I found a paper cup, and without a second thought reached for the pot and began pouring — but the pot froze in midair. Two singular brown drops hung onto the lip of the coffeepot, desperate to fling themselves into my cup, but they were the last drops of the pot.

"Huh?" was the only sound that escaped my dry lips, but my rebellious spirit was not as slow as my words. At that moment I felt a seed of irritation quickly plant itself in the pit of my stomach.

How dare someone take the last cup and not make a fresh pot, I thought, watering the irate seed just a little. *Maybe I'll skip mak-*

ing that first pot tomorrow morning! my mind added, throwing on a bit of fertilizer.

I was usually the first to arrive at the office and on most mornings was glad to make the initial pot of coffee in order to grab my first cup. I generally like a second cup with my lunch. This was not the first time I'd come to the pot at noon only to find an empty carafe. Rattling the cabinet doors a bit more than necessary, I prepared a fresh pot of coffee.

"Hey, you making a pot? Great! I took the last cup about an hour ago and can use another one," a new coworker stated, coming around the corner.

I could feel my seed rapidly sprout tall. Anger was just about to blossom. "You took the last cup? Why didn't you make a fresh pot?"

From the look on my coworker's face, I could see that my voice must have been generously laced with the annoyance I could barely control.

"Well, I guess I never thought about it. The coffee always seems to be here and I never had to make it before."

Do you think the coffee fairy comes to make the coffee? I thought, but I had the good sense to hold my tongue. "It really isn't hard. Premeasured coffee packets are in this drawer, the filters are in the cabinet, and once you fill the machine you simply flip this switch." I emphasized my point by doing just that.

"Thanks, I'll be sure to fill it up the next time," she remarked, heading back to her desk.

As I stood next to the pot, waiting for my precious brew, I carefully contemplated both her attitude and mine. Perhaps she should have been more considerate, but was I really justified in my response toward her careless behavior? I could feel my thorny anger plant begin to wither. Perhaps her action was thoughtless, I confessed, but it was certainly not deliberate. Again, I felt a jab inside my gut as the plant's roots began to shrivel.

And even if it *had* been deliberate, would that have justified my rudeness? Jesus taught that we are to do good to those who do us evil. He then provided us with the best example the universe could hold — he died for sins he did not commit. He took our death sentence.

I think I'll make both morning and afternoon pots of coffee tomorrow. Sure beats the aftertaste left by that dead anger plant.

See that no one renders evil for evil to anyone, but always pursue what is good.

1 Thessalonians 5:15 NKJV

32

purple coffee?

If you ask a hundred people to tell you their favorite color, I doubt that even one would choose the color brown. Blue, yellow, pink, and purple will all be chosen long before brown. Personally, I like brown. It is a strong color—the color of sequoia tree trunks and rich fertile soil. The color of Grandma's tortoise shell hairbrush, Noah's ark, and, of course, coffee beans! Coffee just would not taste the same if it were not brown. I do not even want to imagine what hot purple coffee would taste like! Yuck. The Old Testament Hebrew word for *brown* comes from a root word meaning "warm." Could there be a better color for coffee? Watching the snow fall on a frigid winter's eve would not be as cozy with a hot purple beverage.

Children know what to do with a brown crayon. Brown crayons are for mountains, teddy bears, and cows that give chocolate milk. Songs may praise our country's purple mountains' majesty, but be assured that few children want to color their magnificent hills with a purple crayon. When you give an assortment of crayons to little Suzy, purple is the color used for the bully's shirt and the monster under the bed. Grass is green, the sky is blue, and the sun is colored a gloriously brilliant yellow. Kids know what color is right for each slice of their world.

Brown is an excellent color for clothing, especially for boys and for men who would rather watch football than attend a gala opening. It's not a fussy color. A few stray crumbs and a spot of salsa will hardly be noticed on a brown sweatshirt. Women can safely sport slimming brown slacks. Marilyn Monroe knew the value of brown coffee. When the date of her wedding to famous playwright Arthur Miller was moved forward, she found herself with no veil to match her fawn-colored gown. She did the only logical thing; she took a pot of extra-strong coffee and soaked a white veil in this amazing elixir. Voilà! A matching veil soon emerged.

Have you ever wondered what brown would smell like? I have little doubt that it would smell like coffee laced with chocolate and cinnamon. That seems to me the perfect concoction of scents for the color brown. Rich, spicy, and sweet—oh, yes!

You may snicker at my love for this unapplauded, often-forgotten, and less-than-brilliant pigment, but God knew exactly what he was doing when he created the many shades of brown that adorn this universe. When God spoke our earth into existence, he needed a color that was stable and trustworthy. He dressed his creation with a solid comfortable base coat of brown. Then he dabbed a few bright highlights over the top to keep our attention.

Brown is not depressing or dull. It's sturdy and distinct. Brown is not a hue *lacking* color; it is a hue *full* of color. Mix all of the primary shades together in random proportions and you will not get black—you will get chocolate brown. It is every color of the rainbow thrown together in human fashion. A blending of light and dark, warm and cool.

The Almighty is not a God of disorder. Each and every aspect of our universe was carefully planned and created with

82

perfection. Yes, even the humble color of the coffee bean was not an accident. It was a color engineered by the greatest engineer of them all — God.

Then God saw everything that He had made, and indeed it was very good.

Genesis 1:31 NKJV

33

yum!

Hard as I tried, I could not keep my mind on my work. I'd been chipping away at a mountain of folders for hours, and their grinning flaps had begun to mock me. I needed a coffee break.

Picking up the phone, I dialed the extension of a colleague. "Hey, feel like taking a break?" I asked, trying to keep a pleading tone out of my voice.

Her formal greeting quickly changed to a more casual tone as she responded, "Sorry. Can't. I had a meeting all morning and just got back . . . but if you're heading for the cafeteria, you might want to check out the new French vanilla cappuccino! It's really good."

As I hung up the phone I thought I detected the scent of vanilla wafting up from the cafeteria two floors below. "Come . . . taste me!" it called.

I arose from my chair, anticipation also rising within me. Then the phone rang. *I'll just take this one quick call,* I thought. But that was not to be.

Twenty minutes and two phone calls later, I made another attempt to get myself a cup of the recommended French vanilla coffee. This time I was intercepted halfway to the elevator. Returning to my desk with my captor, I retrieved his needed information and made a few notes for clarification before trying for the cafeteria once again.

By this time, not only could I sense the aroma of vanilla, but the very essence of the coffee seemed to have crept onto my taste buds. I did not just want a cup of this coffee—I craved it. My desire for that French vanilla cappuccino had turned into a roaring, fire-breathing dragon I could not slay. My passion needed to be fed, and feed it I would.

I almost ran to the cafeteria this time, trotting down the three flights of stairs like a young colt in a new green field. I vaguely remember a familiar friendly voice calling my name, but I made a conscious decision to turn in the other direction, feigning deafness.

When I finally reached the machine, I grabbed a cup, thrust it under the spout, and with more joy than was appropriate for this situation, I pushed the button and waited for the rich caramel-colored liquid to froth forth. But nothing happened. I pushed the button again. Still nothing. I gave the machine a little shove and pushed the button yet one more time—really hard. Nothing.

Words that hadn't come to mind for many years suddenly returned to memory. Then I saw the little sign placed ever so smartly at the side of the machine—OUT OF ORDER.

In the blink of an eye, that small placard took every drop of joy out of my body. Flattened like a two-week-old balloon, I returned to my desk with a cup of plain black java.

Lord, why did you let me get my hopes up if you weren't going to let me have what I desired? I thought.

Ever so gently, like a kiss drifting from the clouds, the Father spoke to my spirit. "Take a good look at your desire and see it for what it is."

85

Ouch. I'd set aside my work responsibilities, avoided a good friend, and allowed thoughts into my brain that never would have come if I hadn't been so fixated on that coffee. I know that one of the Father's greatest pleasures is to give his children good gifts. The key, I think, is in the definition of what is good.

"But seek first the kingdom of God and His righteousness, and all these things shall be added to you."

Matthew 6:33 NKJV

34

boston tea

Turning his face from those mingling in the town square, the Patriot rubbed his weather-beaten hands together and then blew into their cupped form to warm himself. Stomping his feet to aid circulation as well as to cover the whisper of his words, the middle-aged farmer spoke to his young neighbor, "Have you heard? The ship *Polly* is not a three-decker like they first thought. The *Gazette* says she's a black ship with no head or ornaments."

"Yes, I heard that as well," his friend whispered in return, the December cold making his words visible in the frosty air.

He stole a glance across the square. Over his friend's shoulder he saw a group of red-coated British officers. "You heard the plan?" he asked through clenched teeth.

"Yes. The last 'tea party' for these parts is set."

"My wife has chosen to brew coffee each day in place of our tea. I have taken a true liking to that black brew," the young man reflected.

"I too have grown fond of the dear beverage. It is strong and lifts the spirit. The taste of tea now only reminds me of the king's greed and tyranny." For a moment the older gent's voice held just a touch of sadness.

But a huge grin spread across the rough unshaven face of the younger man as he rubbed his hand against his whiskers. "Got to get me a shave. Those injuns are all clean faced, ain't they?"

"Not me. We need only appear as such to the bystander, but the shipmen must accurately inform the British that they dealt with Patriots," the farmer said, again blowing into his hands. "We must only disguise ourselves enough to protect our families."

"Ye may be right. Even now we have left little doubt where we stand regarding taxation. King George will know." He looked over the other man's shoulder at the British soldier coming their way and nodded his head ever so slightly in that direction.

"It will be dangerous in any case. Do not be careless or we could lose men," the older man cautioned softly.

Speaking just above a whisper now, the younger one responded, "I will not act foolishly. But know that each and every man I bring with me is ready to give his life." Realizing the nearness of the soldier, the young man suddenly raised his voice so as to be clearly heard. "Guess I'll see you at the 'gathering' then. Good day, neighbor."

The men clasped hands and parted just as the unsuspecting enemy passed their way.

The freedom to decide what we will do and whom we will serve is dear to Americans. Through the centuries, individuals have given up many things for those rights. Tea would still be the beverage of choice in this country if it were not for the powerful need of men to make their own choices. From the beginning of time, God wanted humans to choose freely. The decision to drink coffee instead of tea may seem rather trivial today, but it impacted the economy of nations and the people of this country for decades. Yes, we have the right to make our own decisions, but will we choose correctly? At times I feel it is a bother to approach God with trifling matters that need attention. I have found, however, that no decision is so small that God should be left out of it. Like the loving Father that he is, God is always there to help me make good choices for myself and others around me.

If any of you is lacking in wisdom, ask God, who gives to all generously and ungrudgingly, and it will be given you.

James 1:5

35

the waitress

The petite young waitress approached me with a smile as bright as the neon lighting shimmering off the Formica tabletops.

"May I help you?" she asked with just a hint of a grin still playing around the edges of her mouth as she pulled out her pen and pad.

I handed her the unopened menu and responded, "Yes, I'll have a dish of your rice pudding and black coffee . . . and I'm a bit short on time," I added quickly.

Her smile flashed in full force once again. "Sure. I'll get that for you right away."

True to her word, she returned with a hot cup of coffee and a dish of rice pudding laced with whipped cream and nutmeg. "Let me know if you need anything else," she said over her shoulder as she headed off to handle the rest of the crowd. Something in her voice told me that this was not idle waitress talk. I knew that all I had to do was call out her name and she would take care of whatever I needed.

As I sipped my coffee, I pulled out some meeting notes needing review, but my attention would not stay with the task. It was repeatedly drawn to this diner's enthusiastic waitress. Apparently her pleasant nature had nothing to do with my compelling personality. She seemed more than happy to fulfill the request of every patron, courteous or surly.

As I drained my cup, the young woman unfailingly returned, pot in hand. Despite the busy dinner crowd, she always managed to flash that smile and share a moment of conversation. She laughed when I urged her to fill the cup to the brim and then asked me if I'd always taken my coffee black. "Real coffee lovers seem to start off with cream or sugar but eventually they graduate to black," she revealed.

I liked this young lady. Not only was she a fellow coffee lover, but she waited on tables with quick efficiency. She also understood that her job was more than serving up meals. A good server delivers comfort to the soul and joy to the spirit. My waitress, Kira, seemed to grasp this instinctively. Our momentary connection made the simple act of filling my cup one of friendship.

I do not know if this young woman will be a diner waitress for one day or for many years to come. I do know that no matter where she goes or what she does, her attitude and gracious manner will be a credit to her.

I also do not know if Kira is a Christian, but her attitude is one that Christians can and should respect. Enthusiasm, genuine caring, and hard work are all attributes Jesus asks us to demonstrate in everything we do. We are to act as if Jesus is the recipient of our actions. Kira's willingness to be a servant made me shameful of my own occasional lack of enthusiasm when asked to serve. I know that Jesus would have been pleased with the service I received at the Ringwood Diner — I sure was.

Render service with enthusiasm, as to the Lord and not to men and women.

Ephesians 6:7

36

italian wine cake
surprise

The moment my son's friend opened the car door, I recognized the gift he was holding. Its scent struggled from within the folds of foil that covered it and reached my nostrils with tempting abandon. My quick grin brought me a return of the same from the young man. He knew the welcome his mom's Italian Wine Cake would receive at my house.

"Hey! Is that a cake?" my strapping six-foot-four teenager asked, craning his neck from the backseat. "What kind?"

"Yes, it is . . . and I believe Tom's mother made it for *me*, so it really doesn't matter what kind it is," I joked.

"Aw, I know you're going to share," he added, putting on his most engaging smile.

"Sure, I'll share," I replied. "It's just that I've seen your idea of a portion, and I would very much like to taste this cake . . . not just its crumbs."

"I just want one piece," he quipped. "I've had Mrs. Mackwell's cakes and I don't want to get left out of this deal."

Looking in my rearview mirror as I backed out of the driveway, I could see the two young men grinning at me like a pair of Cheshire cats. The cake, which sat on my front seat, continued to permeate the atmosphere with its aroma. When we arrived at the school, my son exited the car, allowing his last words to hang in the air as the door closed behind him, "Don't forget to save me a piece of that cake!"

I had to laugh at the forsaken look he threw me as I drove off.

Once home I tossed my coat across the back of a kitchen chair and headed straight for the coffeepot. While the coffee brewed I unwrapped my luscious treasure.

"Ah!" I sighed.

Now completely unencumbered by its cover, the aroma of the still-warm cake mingled with the robust bouquet of the coffee. Could this be the scent of heaven? Drawn from my dream by the sound of footsteps, I greeted my husband as he emerged from our basement.

"Hi, hon," I said, waiting for the customary peck on the cheek.

Instead he offered, "Hmm, what's that? You making a pot of coffee? And what is that other wonderful smell?"

"Lynn made us one of her Italian Wine Cakes! Doesn't it smell good?" I replied, turning my attention back to the cake.

No sooner did the words fall across my lips than my son Alan miraculously appeared from down the hall.

"What's that? Cake?" he asked.

Seeming not to need an answer, he began getting out plates, forks, and a knife. I sliced the moist cake into generous servings and quickly dished it up—careful to set aside some for my youngest as promised. Coffee seemed the perfect accompaniment to the rich spices in this cake, and I savored each bite.

What made this cake so special? Perhaps it is because all of Lynn's recipes seem to be chosen with multiple senses in mind. The smell, texture, and appearance of her cakes have been honed to a fine art. But I also think that our love for her baked goods stems from their presentation. She does not usually bake a cake for a person's birthday. She bakes cakes "just because," and they appear on your doorstep without warning. Lynn definitely has a talent in the kitchen, but her greatest talent is that she's learned to share her abundance throughout the year. Lynn, you are a blessing!

And God is able to provide you with every blessing in abundance, so that by always having enough of everything, you may share abundantly in every good work.

2 Corinthians 9:8

children's coffee

My second grader, Alan, sat at the kitchen table eating his breakfast. I was on the phone with a neighbor, making carpool arrangements for Saturday's soccer game while trying to keep my eye on the clock.

"Alan, hurry and finish your coffee, then get in to brush your teeth before you miss the bus," I said. Alan took a last gulp as he pushed his chair back and headed down the hallway.

An incredulous voice on the other end of the line broke into my thoughts. "I know I could not have heard you right. You aren't letting your kids drink coffee, are you?"

"Well, it's not *black* coffee. It's more like milk flavored with coffee," I responded, just a little irritated.

"Really? Aren't you worried about letting them have the caffeine? Do you know how bad that could be for him?"

Answering her question with a question, I asked, "Don't you let your kids have cola drinks, and doesn't your family drink a pitcher of iced tea with dinner each evening?"

"Well, sure . . ."

I continued, not allowing her to fully respond. "Do you know that a glass of iced tea has just as much caffeine, more sugar, and a whole lot less nutrition than the cup of half milk and half coffee that Alan had with breakfast? Do you know that a single can of cola can eat away the paint from the surface of a car and that the aluminum that leaches into the cola from the can is being investigated as a possible cause of Alzheimer's disease? And do you also know that the steam that rises from a single cup of coffee has more cancer-fighting antioxidants than three oranges?"

"Uh, no, I didn't know any of that," said my neighbor. "I think I've got to go now. I'll call you later," she added quickly. Click.

How quick we are to judge each other. What may be perfectly acceptable in one culture may be abhorrent in another. I grew up in a German home. Although it may seem strange to Americans, German children are brought up on coffee the same way that an English child is served tea or an American child is served hot cocoa. Their children's coffee is usually half milk or cream and the other half coffee. Although this caffeine content is comparable to that of a traditional chocolate bar or cola drink, Americans still consider coffee inappropriate for children.

Just as one group of people may judge another's cultural habits to be wrong, Christians are sometimes critical of one another's denominational practices. One may kneel to pray and others may rise and raise their hands. Pentecostals clap their hands and sway to the sound of drums and brass instruments; Methodists sit solemnly while a choir sings accompanied by an organ; and Quakers choose no accompaniment and sing their hymns a cappella.

Each group has a reason why they worship in their chosen manner, but I believe that God is much less concerned with their choice of music and manner of presentation than he is with the state of their hearts. When we are quick to judge one another, we build walls that hinder relationships.

It took a while before I could approach my neighbor with the same level of friendship I felt before our coffee conversation. We managed to tear down the wall we built between us, but how much easier it would have been if we'd both chosen not to build it in the first place. I hope that believers in Christ can set aside those things that are not matters of salvation. Our job is to build bridges, not to set up walls.

Therefore let us not judge one another anymore, but rather resolve this, not to put a stumbling block or a cause to fall in our brother's way.

Romans 14:13 NKJV

38

saguaro cactus love

I sat in a small Phoenix café drinking Mexican coffee while waiting for my sister to arrive. The strange and wonderful terrain of the desert intrigued me to no end. Coming from the lush, green, pine barrens of the northeast, this exotic place with its unfamiliar plant life and lung-sucking dry air was exciting.

The huge window at the rear of the café overlooked a beautiful cactus garden. I always thought that deserts were stark and lonely—places of death—but staring out this window I was assaulted by sights that screamed just the opposite. Flowers bloomed, small lizards scurried, and from somewhere I could hear the unusual call of a bird. It sounded a little like my car on a cold winter in New Jersey—*chuah-chuah-chuah*.

"Something interesting?" my sister Helga asked, smiling when she arrived. This was a rather silly question since she knew that I found everything I saw on this my first visit to Phoenix interesting.

"Can you believe that bird?" I asked incredulously. "It's building a nest in that big prickly cactus."

"That's a saguaro," she said, picking up her menu as if her statement was self-explanatory.

"The cactus or the bird?" I asked, solidifying my greenhorn status.

"Huh? Oh! The cactus." Setting down her menu, she looked with more interest at the huge green tower. "That saguaro cactus has to be at least a hundred years old. See the arms? Saguaros don't grow arms until they reach a hundred. Most live between 125 and 175 years. Some live to be 300 years old. That bird flying back and forth to its arm is a cactus wren. It's building a nest in the arm . . . see?"

"Amazing! It's actually going to live in the middle of those sharp cactus needles?" I rubbed my arm where I'd felt the sting of just such a needle that morning.

"Well, it probably isn't going to live *there*. Cactus wrens build a lot of nests to fool their predators, but they only use one of them. Chances are that is just one of its decoys." Helga returned to her menu, but I could not take my eyes off the industrious little, brown bird.

God was so amazing. Here was a tiny, brown bird not much different from the average sparrow. This creature certainly wasn't anything special. Its song was not beautiful by any stretch of the imagination and could even be called somewhat annoying. Its plumage did not turn heads. But God cared for it. He provided an unusual but perfect place to keep this small creature safe.

Now the cactus wren could have argued that, being denied the brilliant colors of the peacock or the beautiful song of the nightingale, it should at least be given better accommodations. Instead it graciously accepted its home in the saguaro.

You see, the cactus wren knows something many humans haven't figured out. Adversity is not always a bad thing. Raising your fledglings in the midst of sharp cactus needles produces just the right amount of caution and strength. Even with the safety that the saguaro's sharp needles provide, the bird goes one step further. It willingly works to build numerous decoy nests. If thorns do not deter a predator, it may still find itself empty-handed with the cactus wren looking on from a safe distance.

Living with trials can be difficult, but they can ultimately be for our own good.

He delivers the afflicted by their affliction, and opens their ear by adversity.

Job 36:15

39

pumpkin bread
coffee cans

I poured the last of the sumptuously fragrant ground coffee from its tin and into my storage container. Staring at the three empty cans before me, I could not prevent the grin that spread across my face. Thanksgiving was right around the corner, and now I could get ready.

Three empty coffee cans may not herald the coming of Thanksgiving for most people, but they do for me. They are the first step in preparing my pumpkin bread. The pumpkin bread recipe I received from a good friend many years ago calls for the batter to be baked in one-pound coffee cans. The final product slips out of its cylindrical pan and slices into perfect circles of a moist, raisin-and-walnut-filled breakfast delight. I'm not the best cook in the world, but this is one recipe that seems to work for me. Not only is it delicious, but its unusual appearance makes a beautiful presentation.

Certainly in some cases, appearances can be deceiving. A delicacy that at first looks tempting may well taste awful. About a year ago I stopped at a new bakery on my way to work. I wanted to pick up a few pastries to celebrate the birthday of a colleague. Everything in the store looked wonderful, and although it wasn't easy I eventually chose my baked goods, including a butter horn generously adorned with almonds and what appeared to be coarse sugar. After presenting the surprise to our birthday girl, a number of us grabbed a mug of coffee and helped ourselves. I chose the almond horn.

As our group sat in the cafeteria ready to appreciate our small indulgence, I took my first bite of the pastry. To my horror I found that someone had used coarse salt instead of sugar to top the delicacy. It was awful!

People can be like that too. Our appearance can enhance what is inside of us and, like the pumpkin bread, add to the pleasure of those around us. They are initially attracted to us by what they see, and as they enjoy our company they find even more delight in the richness of who we are.

Other people are more like the wrongly baked almond horn. Some individuals spend a great deal of time making sure that their outsides are attractive, but not enough time making sure the inside ingredients are right. When their colleagues and neighbors get to know them, the truth becomes evident. Their sweet appearance gives way to the salty taste of who they really are.

I hope that when someone meets me they do not find me physically or socially unacceptable. But more than that, I hope that Christ's Spirit within me makes them come back to find out more about what I'm really made of.

Do not adorn yourselves outwardly by braiding your hair, and by wearing gold ornaments or fine clothing; rather, let your adornment be the inner self with the lasting beauty of a gentle and quiet spirit, which is very precious in God's sight.

1 Peter 3:3–4

40

new orleans
and chicory coffee

New Orleans feeds on its nightlife; I am a morning person. These two things don't usually make for a good mix, unless you are looking for a special blend of coffee — New Orleans style.

My husband and I walked hand in hand down the nearly deserted streets of the New Orleans French Quarter. We could hear the peculiar sound of a trumpet as it echoed through the morning from one of the all-night bars. The sunrise had already taken the chill off of the morning, and the air was beginning to warm our bare arms. Other than the two of us, the only life seemed to be conscientious storekeepers who washed down the cobblestone streets and walkways leading to their shops.

Partly due to my longing for a good cup of coffee, and in some measure because my husband's family bears the name DuMont, we were headed toward the Café du Monde for a serving of their famous beignets and some chicory coffee. Open twenty-four hours a day, the establishment was not without patrons when we arrived.

We were seated in the historic outdoor café across from Jackson Square. Requesting a menu brought a smile and short verbal list of their offerings. The first item on the list was du Monde's chicory coffee, offered black or au lait (laced with warm milk). If coffee was not to your liking, they did serve orange juice and milk. Their deep-fried beignets were the only solid food.

We ordered coffee and beignets. When they arrived, the beignets were covered in powdered sugar, like little snow-covered mountains. Feather light, yet deeply satisfying, the beignets were the perfect accompaniment to the chicory coffee. Normally I'm not in favor of adulterating my morning coffee with anything but good old coffee beans, but their blend was no less than perfect. Chicory, a root of the endive plant, was first used in coffee by the French during their civil war. When this root is roasted, ground, and added to coffee, it tends to soften the bitter edge of dark roasted beans. It also adds what one could describe as a hint of chocolate flavor to the brew.

Now, I'll admit that my husband had to talk me into trying this coffee. I don't believe in messing around with what I already know is a good thing. But once I tried it, I liked it.

Some Christians shy away from other believers who may worship in a different style or choose to live or dress in some unusual way. Like the chicory coffee, we may shy away from something we aren't familiar with. But good coffee is good coffee. So long as we all profess Christ as our Savior, I say, enjoy the diversity!

So we who are many, are one body in Christ, and individually we are members one of another.

Romans 12:5

41

ticktock, ticktock

I remember the days of summer passing ever so slowly when I was a child. Even with farm chores, I managed to find endless hours for picking wild strawberries and organizing elaborate costume plays and festivals with any unwitting childhood companion willing to get involved. Then, of course, there were those hours when we simply lay on our backs in the tall grass, imagining wooly bears and blazing pirate ships passing in the clouds overhead.

My father once told me that as you get older, time passes more quickly. It is like an old watch whose spring begins to wear out and in desperation pushes the hands faster. I laughed when he told me . . . but I'm not laughing now.

My days are filled from early morning until late in the evening, yet I never seem to get done half of what I need to do, and only a smidgen of what I want to do. In order to make the most of every minute, I stick to a pretty tight routine. I arrive at the office at least half an hour before the start of my workday, where I put on a pot of coffee and spend a few moments with my devotional before getting to work. One morning a few weeks ago, a coworker suggested we take a quick walk around the building to get some morning exercise. I hesitated only a moment and then agreed.

For the next few days, my routine was to start the coffee and then go for a walk — prayer and devotion time didn't seem to fit into my schedule anymore. I still had time to catch a cup of coffee when I got back, and I intended to arrive earlier so I wouldn't miss my time with the Lord, but every day some new reason kept me from getting out of the house sooner. I truly enjoyed the morning exercise and the social time, and I just couldn't seem to do it all.

That was when my life started crumbling. A friend at church lost his job, another became seriously ill, and a third was on the brink of divorce. I wanted to pray for them — and I did think of them often — but I just did not have a set time for prayer.

One morning my walking partner called in sick. Walking alone wasn't nearly as much fun, so I returned to my desk and cracked open my devotional for the first time in months. The verses that jumped out were Luke 22:31–32. Ouch!

I thought about all the times I was too weak to pray but others faithfully lifted my troubles up to God for me. I remembered the many crises that were averted because my mother faithfully stayed on her knees. I pondered the faithful martyrs who would not turn away when ordered to stop praying. I felt ashamed and humbled that God would consider me at all worthy to approach him after ignoring him for so long. I bowed my head and asked forgiveness, then tenderly lifted up each person God brought to mind.

When my coworker returned to work the next day, I suggested we take our walks at lunchtime. She readily agreed. I still don't have more hours in each day, but I've learned that even when your time is limited, you can still make time for the important things. Now I make time for my coffee, my prayer, and my exercise . . . not necessarily in that order.

Satan has asked for you, that he may sift you as wheat. But I have prayed for you.

Luke 22:31–32 NKJV

42

a coffee bath

We'd only lived in our new home for a few weeks when it happened. It was September and Indian summer came on us with a vengeance. Each afternoon my third grader took advantage of the warm weather by exploring his new neighborhood. The pond near our house turned into his favorite fishing hole, and the neighborhood boys became kick-ball teammates and adventurous cohorts.

Each evening I'd have him jump into the tub to remove the layers of grime applied during his afternoon explorations.

On this day, I absentmindedly started the tub water, then turned to ready the towels and care for other matters.

"Let's go J. C., bath time. You still have homework to do after dinner," I called to my reluctant young man.

"Okay, Mom," he replied, shuffling in as I headed out of the bathroom.

Then it hit.

"Hey! I'm not taking a bath in this!"

"What are you talking about?" I called back over my shoulder.

"Really, Mom, I *can't* take a bath in this! Come here!"

Prepared for some lame excuse, I returned to the bathroom. Eyes wide, I watched as my tub filled with what appeared to be a batch of weak coffee.

"What is that?" I asked my son as if he was responsible.

"I didn't do anything. Honest!" he protested. "I just came in here and that stuff was coming out of the faucet!"

In shock, I turned off the water and stood motionless. Gratefully, my quick-witted son recovered his good sense.

"Hey, call next door and see if they have yucky water too!" J. C. quipped.

One of the neighborhood's longtime residents had been particularly friendly, so I decided to give her a call in hopes that she would have some answers.

"Carol? Hi. I just ran the tub for J. C. and—"

"Oh, no!" Carol interrupted. "I should have called you. They just flushed the water mains, and your water is going to look awful for a day or so. It's just minerals and the like. There is nothing harmful in the water. We've had it tested a number of times just to be sure."

"How often do they do this?" I asked, still concerned.

"Around twice a year, and like I said, it only lasts a day or so. Do you get the local paper?"

"No . . ."

"Well, if you decide to subscribe, they tell you when the town will flush them. Oh, one more thing . . . you don't want to do any wash when the water is like this."

After some polite chitchat, we said good-bye and I returned to the bathroom where my son stared at the opaque water.

"Drain the water out of the tub," I told him. "Just close your eyes and take a quick shower instead of a bath."

J. C.'s jaw dropped. "You mean you want me to shower in this stuff?" he asked incredulously.

Staring at the remnants of the afternoon kick-ball game that still clung to his skinny legs, I replied, "Yup . . . and . . . use the old brown towel, not our good white ones."

As I returned to the kitchen, I wondered what I could make for dinner that did not require the use of water. "J. C.? Make that shower quick. As soon as your father gets home, we're going out for dinner."

We've lived in that house for over fifteen years, and now I faithfully watch the newspaper for the semiannual flushing of the water mains. I wasn't prepared the first time the water turned brown, but I am now. Even though we have long periods of time when our delicious, community well water is crystal clear, I know to keep my eyes open for the day when coffee-colored water will again run from our tap.

Some people have been warned that Christ will return. They too say it's been a long time since he came and it certainly isn't going to happen today. I wonder if they will be as surprised as I was when my tap water turned brown.

Therefore prepare your minds for action; discipline yourselves; set all your hope on the grace that Jesus Christ will bring you when he is revealed.

1 Peter 1:13

43

evacuation

When the alarm sounded, I was caught off guard. The open packet of premeasured coffee that I held dropped to the floor, creating mottled brown designs on our blue corporate carpet. As my coworkers spilled out of their offices and hurried toward the stairway, I dropped to my knees and with the aid of a few paper towels attempted to clean up the mess. *It's only a drill*, I thought. *What's the harm in cleaning up the mess first?*

Scooping up the grounds as best I could, I tossed the waste into the trash just as the security guard came upon me.

"Are you still here? You need to evacuate the building," he said in a stern voice.

"I know. I'm sorry. When the alarm went off it startled me and I dumped coffee grounds all over the place. It took longer than I thought to clean it up," I said calmly, pointing to the shadow of coffee still evident on the carpet.

The guard frowned, obviously affronted by my lack of discomfort at remaining behind. I set my handful of paper towels down on the counter then started back to my desk.

"Where are you going? The exit is this way." He shot steelbound words at me even as he covered the area between us in record time. This guy meant business.

"I, umm, was just going back to my desk to get my purse,"

I replied as casually as I could over the sound of the still blaring alarm.

With an arm gently but firmly on my elbow, he turned me toward the stairwell. "You've got to exit the building. I'll make sure everything up here is secure."

No longer willing to protest, I hurried down the stairs and out of the building.

"You just getting out? Where were you?" a friend asked as I joined the group at the rear of the parking lot.

"Oh, I was making a pot of coffee and I spilled the grounds. Didn't want to leave the mess . . . actually, I wouldn't have come out at all except that the guard found me as I was finishing up. He insisted!" I added, placing my hand on my hip.

My friend responded with no sympathy for me whatsoever. "What's the matter with you? Once the drill is over you can always go back and clean up. What if there was a real fire or a bomb in the building? You think the danger would disappear simply because you didn't think it was real?"

Just then the alarm stopped and the guards began motioning the employees to return to the building. "See! It's only a drill!" I protested.

"You didn't know that for sure," she shot back. "There are some things people just shouldn't take chances with."

When I got back to my desk, I took a moment to reflect on my friend's advice. She was right, of course; there are some things a person should not take chances with.

Where we will spend eternity after we leave this earth is one of those things. It occurs to me that many people treat their salvation the same way I treated the evacuation drill. Bad things only happen to someone else, and there will be plenty of time to check out God issues later. Unfortunately, that isn't always the case. If you have not taken God's promises of heaven and hell seriously, perhaps you should.

See, now is the acceptable time; see, now is the day of salvation!

2 Corinthians 6:2

44

coffee stains

Both my husband and I were fed up with the horrible old carpet in our living room. It took quite a while for us to save enough money to purchase new living-room furniture. Now the carpet's heavy antique gold color mocked the light grays and steel blue shades of our couch.

"What color carpet do you think we should get for the living room and hall?" I asked my husband, who was busy working the newspaper crossword puzzle.

"Umm . . . whatever you think is fine with me," he answered, not even looking up.

Thus began my search for the perfect carpet. I stopped at every department and carpet store I came across. I carefully compared yarn swatches, color chips, and padding types. You would not believe how many choices I had. Unable to decide on the color or style, I approached one saleswoman who turned out to be quite helpful. She started by asking me what the carpeted room would be used for. Then she asked how many kids we had, whether they were boys or girls, and what sort of entertainment our family enjoyed.

After patiently noting my answers, she directed me to a lovely caramel and gray carpet that contained scattered specs of brown, blue, and black. It was perfect. With three growing boys who were constantly inviting friends over, I felt this dust- and ash-colored carpet would hide a substantial amount of long-term damage.

We've had that carpet for almost ten years now. My oldest son is married and my other two have grown into men. My carpet has seen dozens of young boys building plastic brick forts and holding intergalactic peace conferences. It has been the home of teen Super Bowl parties, a "you're-turning-forty" Mexican fiesta, indoor Easter egg hunts, and bridal shower preparations. Masses of long-legged teenagers have strewn their bodies across it for Monopoly tournaments, video screenings, and popcorn fights. We've even braved a few splatters of blood from a roller-blade accident, and a number of coffee spills.

Only days after we had the carpet installed, I generously christened it. I was enjoying a hot cup of coffee and watching the Saturday morning news. Our cat, Twinkie, was experiencing one of her "fun" moments. Chasing some imaginary beast, she raced into the room, did a full lap around my chair, then as if launched from a trampoline, she propelled herself into my lap. The coffee mug flew from my hand, splattering its contents all over the carpet. That ended my brief moment of Saturday morning bliss. I quickly grabbed a roll of paper towels from the kitchen along with some soda water and began sponging.

True to the saleswoman's word, the carpet's unique color scheme along with the wonder of stain-guarded fibers worked like a miracle. Within minutes no evidence of the mishap remained.

As believers, when we confess our sin to God, our sin vanishes in the midst of his mercy and grace just the way the coffee stains vanished into the colors of our carpet. Yet, when God makes our sin disappear, it is much more than camouflage. God doesn't just hide the stain; Jesus' sacrifice so completely removes our sin that it is as if we never sinned in the first place. God provided me with the perfect carpet solution for my family, but even better than that, he provided all of humanity with the perfect solution for sin.

As far as the east is from the west, so far he removes our transgressions from us.

Psalm 103:12

45

tall tales

O w!" I cried, fanning my tongue with one hand while trying to keep from spilling the coffee held in the other.

"I told you it was hot," my husband all too patiently remarked.

"You didn't say it was going to take a dozen layers off my tongue!" I replied with my mouth wide open to catch a cool breeze.

"Oh, Mom. There you go again! You know it didn't *really* take any layers off your tongue," my son Tim responded, rolling his eyes as only a six-foot-four sixteen-year-old can.

"How do you know?" I defended myself. "And so what if I exaggerate once in a while. It's not as if others don't know that writers 'color' their speech. Haven't you ever heard of literary license?"

Tim's older brother, Alan, chimed in, "It's one thing to exaggerate when you're writing fiction, Mom, but you have developed a bad habit of stretching the truth in every conversation."

"What are you talking about? I've told you a million times that I never stretch the truth!"

All three men in the room raised their eyebrows. "What? Oh, you're all annoyed because I said 'a million times,' aren't you? Well, the truth is that nine times out of ten I don't stretch the truth at all."

Alan turned to Tim and just shrugged his shoulders. "She's hopeless!" he sighed.

"Now what? You don't think that I can keep from exaggerating? Well let me tell you something . . . um . . . I can. You just watch," I sputtered, afraid to say more.

I stomped to the kitchen and began opening and closing cabinet doors rather loudly.

"What's for dinner?" my teenager asked, strolling into the kitchen.

"Food," I replied a bit more curtly than I wanted to.

"I know that! What are you making?"

"I thought I'd make chicken lips and lizard gills," I replied before I could stop myself.

"Really! That sounds interesting!" He grinned from ear to ear as he headed back into the living room, encouraging his brother back into the fray. "Hey, Alan, guess what? Since Mom isn't exaggerating anymore, she's *really* making chicken lips and lizard gills for dinner this time. Sounds good, doesn't it?"

Alan eagerly took up the torch and entered the kitchen ready for the competition. "Well, I think you made it through one sentence before exaggerating again. Want to try for two?"

"No," I replied, figuring he couldn't get me with that answer.

As I prepared dinner in silence, God confronted me with what my boys already knew.

But, God, I thought, *I'm not lying. Most of the time I'm just trying to emphasize a point or using some silly expression. It's all in fun!*

My thoughts rang hollow in my head, and the Lord's silence convicted me all the more. Suddenly I could think of many occasions where my "fun" was not as clear as I expected it to be.

Okay, Lord, I get the idea. Maybe I need to be a little more careful with my words, I admitted.

As I pulled out the package of hot dogs I would prepare with the macaroni and cheese, I found myself still trying to justify my words.

Hmm, I wonder if they really do put chicken lips and lizard gills in here. Now wouldn't that be interesting! I thought.

Some people play board games, sports, or computer solitaire . . . I play with words. I enjoy making them dance in ways that stimulate the mind and soul. At times I do a fairly good job, and I thank God often for the gift that allows me to share my stories. But along with the gift comes a responsibility. Until the day they make hot dogs with chicken lips, I think I may have to learn just a bit more restraint.

"I tell you, on the day of judgment you will have to give an account for every careless word you utter."

Matthew 12:36

117

46

windmill punches

A person who enjoys watching the sunrise each morning usu-ally needs a good incentive to stay up past bedtime. For me, two good reasons for late-night adventures are the needs of my children and a pot of good coffee. This past Thanksgiving I was blessed into the wee hours of the morning with both.

My son J. C. and his wife, Roni, came to spend their first Thanksgiving with us this year. Long after the leftovers were packed into their midnight-raidable containers, we sat enjoying slices of pie and cups of coffee in the comfort of our living room. I'm not sure what exactly sparked our sudden need to reminisce, but reminisce we did.

"Hey, do you remember all the wrestling matches we had in this room?" one of my sons asked his brothers.

"Oh, yeah!" my youngest piped in with pride. "I do believe I won most of those."

"No way!" his brothers cried, meeting his challenge.

"The way I remember it," my rather hefty son, Alan, contin-ued, "I usually ended up the winner . . . on top of both of you."

Not to be left out, my eldest, J. C., also entered the fray. "Of course you came out on top, sitting on me was your only defense! You and that roly-poly move you thought was so cool." Not ready to leave the youngest out of his more sophisticated memory, he turned to Tim. "And you! The only reason you *think* you won was because you'd come into the match with your arms flying in every direction while yelling, 'Here comes the windmill punch—watch out!' Then Alan and I would end up on the floor laughing so hard we couldn't breathe!"

At this point my daughter-in-law and I just looked at each other. All three boys, now well over six feet tall and certainly no longer children, were taking this juvenile matter quite seriously.

"I think you should all get together later for a midnight club meeting to discuss this," my husband interjected, his broad grin indicating there was more to this statement than at first seemed evident.

"Midnight club?" was all my daughter-in-law could ask.

I took a thoughtful sip from my coffee cup and smiled. "J. C. and Alan used to have this club. They called it their midnight club. Every night they would plan to meet at midnight. Most of the time they couldn't stay awake, but every once in a while J. C. would rouse himself in the middle of the night and go get his brother." I sipped my coffee once again, remembering the skinny, wild-haired child who was the key player in most of the boys' schemes. "On those mornings we'd find J. C. and Alan sound asleep under the kitchen table, usually with a favorite toy or two tucked under their arms."

With the patience only a new wife can muster, Roni turned to her husband and asked, "And *why* did you do this?"

J. C. and Alan shared a look of profound insight. Then, head held high and chin thrust forward in defiance, J. C. responded to his wife, "Because *we* were members of the midnight club."

It took a few moments for the rest of us to stop laughing, then the banter resumed and the remainder of the evening continued in the same vein. As I cleared away the coffee cups early the next morning, a smile still played around my lips.

119

Joy and fellowship are a part of the very nature of God. I am sure he is thrilled when we share our delight in life and in each other. Don't despair if your circumstances did not leave you with happy childhood memories. Each day God gives us the opportunity to make new memories that can be shared with others in years to come. I am grateful that God gave my children so many wonderful recollections to celebrate, but I hope they won't stop making memories simply because they've grown older. Each day is a new memory waiting to be made.

"I have said these things to you so that my joy may be in you, and that your joy may be complete."

John 15:11

instant comfort

Night had already overtaken the day, and my office building was nearly empty. The quiet was not the pleasant type I experience at the beginning of my day. Morning quiet is full of anticipation and invigorates my soul. This was a long-day, bone-weary kind of quiet. Except for the steady drone of my computer as it created the reports that kept me at my desk, the only sound on this Friday evening was the faint and distant movement of the cleaning staff at the other end of the floor.

Needing something to refresh my concentration, I pulled out an unopened box of gourmet-flavored instant cappuccino. Even its long name with an international flair momentarily energized me. As I spooned the sugary comfort into my mug, I sniffed its mixture of chocolate and spiced coffee. *Not bad,* I thought. *This may be just what I need.*

I poured the hot water atop the mixture. The sweet bouquet wafting up from the cup drove my mind back to the commercial that prompted me to purchase this product. Once again I saw the fireplace flicker invitingly as two lovers gazed into each other's eyes. Coffee mugs firmly in hand, they exchanged intimate conversation. The man gently laid his free hand atop the woman's in a gesture strangely reminiscent of a Cary Grant and Ingrid Bergman movie. We who watched this scene from afar were sure that it was the coffee that made their special moment possible. Without the coffee we could only imagine chaos. The woman would most likely be battling with the kids to do homework while the man grumbled about the bills that sat in piles on the kitchen counter. Ah, if only my cup of coffee could take me to a place without late nights at the office.

I stirred the caramel-colored liquid with great anticipation. Its scent rose to my nostrils, tempting me to take the first sip. I entered the remaining data into my computer and then set my report to print. Now I could enjoy the moment. I picked up the mug, tentatively placing my lips on the rim. Not too hot—good. I took a sip.

The taste was pleasant enough, but it did not miraculously take me away from my difficult report. Where was my instant comfort? Where was the magic it had promised? No miracle here!

Life is full of God's miracles, but a cup of instant coffee will seldom provide them. Miracles are found in the complexities of the universe: the conception of a child, the birthing of a star, and the passing from an earthly life to an eternal one. Miracles are found in the hard things of life: a young boy overcoming the trauma of an alcoholic mother, a woman depriving herself of earthly pleasure to provide for her children, a man giving his life for those he does not know in times of war. Miracles can even be found in simple things: a delicate flower growing on a rocky mountainside or a hymn sung in the stillness of the night.

Do I believe in miracles? Absolutely! I also think that most people are too ready to accept a cheap substitute for the real thing. You will not find miracles bound in a package of instant coffee . . . but if you believe, you might just find an ample supply in the arms of the One True God.

"Truly I tell you, if you say to this mountain, 'Be taken up and thrown into the sea,' and if you do not doubt in your heart, but believe that what you say will come to pass, it will be done for you."

Mark 11:23

122

48

excessive desires

Some things in this world, although wonderful, should be consumed in moderation. Take whipped cream, for instance.

When my husband and I were teenagers, an ice-cream parlor in our town ran a promotion. Anyone who could eat two of their giant ice-cream sundaes would get them both for free. This might not seem like a grand feat for some, but these were no ordinary sundaes. Each giant sundae contained fifteen scoops of very rich ice cream. Five syrupy sweet toppings crowned the scoops, along with mound upon mound of whipped cream. Now imagine one person trying to eat *two* of those!

Back in high school, my husband, John, was a thin and wiry athlete. Consuming calories was what he did best. One day, he was forced to miss both lunch and dinner. His part-time job as a bass guitar player hadn't been the most lucrative employment, and he needed to be creative in order to fill the screaming void in the pit of his stomach.

Hunger took control of his better judgment, and John decided to take the ice-cream parlor up on its challenge. If he ordered the two giant sundaes and finished them, there would be no problem; but if he ordered them and could *not* finish them, he would be expected to pay with money he did not have. There was only one solution — he had to eat them both.

With his plan in hand, John dug into the first sundae the moment it arrived. Fifteen scoops of ice cream disappeared quickly into the ravenous belly of this teenager. He set the spoon down only when the waitress came to clear away his dish. Then, to her surprise, he smiled and ordered the second sundae. Now heads began to turn. Would he be able to finish the second one? Others had attempted the task, but few had crossed the finish line victorious.

The second sundae arrived, flaunting all of its sweetness, and my husband again dipped in with abandon. Spoonfuls of the frozen delight with its thick toppings soon vanished. As the whipped cream slipped from its icy summit into the dish's valley, John's arm moved ever more slowly to ladle the ice cream upward.

Finally, the bottom of the bowl appeared and the only portion of the sundae that remained was a pool of whipped topping floating upon a sea of sweet syrup. Gawkers had appeared around his booth shortly after the second sundae was delivered. Now they cheered him on as the green-hued teen encouraged himself to finish off the remnant.

Days later he confidently reported that the ice cream went down easy. It was the last few spoonfuls of whipped cream that almost did him in. The experience did make him a legend of sorts at our school, but I've noticed that he is no longer a big fan of whipped cream on top of his sundaes.

Espresso is coffee's equivalent of whipped cream. I remember, as a child, staring into my mother's china cabinet. Shimmering on its glass shelves were her delicate, gold-rimmed demitasse cups. I could never understand why she would not let me play with these perfect child-sized cups. Many years later, when I entertained my first cup of espresso, I understood that even adults sometimes need to take a small portion.

Only an adult with little self-control might drink a large mug of espresso or devour bowl upon bowl of whipped cream. I imagine both would soon take revenge on their consumer. God gives generously to his children but cautions us to choose both the quality and quantity wisely. Some things are definitely better in small quantities.

Like a city breached, without walls, is one who lacks self-control.

Proverbs 25:28

49

the good old days

The weather was particularly warm for March that year. I'd grabbed my winter coat out of habit, but when I arrived at work and hung it on its hanger, I realized that the afternoon would bring temperatures far too warm for the covering I'd chosen.

A sigh escaped my lips as I ran my hand down the sleeve of the coat. I'm not really a clotheshorse, but something was particularly nice about this coat. It suited me. Being the sort of person who is always a bit cold, I liked its wool warmth. It was long enough to cover my calves but not so long as to trip me when I hurried through the holiday crowds. Although it buttoned in the front, it just as easily could be worn open to catch the brisk fall air or to feel the refreshing first chill of winter. Now it was almost time to set my friend aside and don an appropriate spring jacket.

For just a moment my mind left the office and I was once again an immigrant child on a New Jersey farm.

"Luisa . . . take the coats and the stiff brush outside. I will bring the coffee," I heard my mother say.

Obediently I did as I was told. Each of our winter coats was hung upon a heavy wooden hanger, and each hanger was hung on the old clothesline strung from the back of the house to the tall metal pole at the back of the yard. Standing on the tips of my toes to reach the top of the coats, I began to brush each from collar to hem with the stiff natural-bristle brush. Every trace of lint and speck of dirt was removed before the dark wool coats were hung with their mothballs in the big storage closet my grandfather had built. When my mother came out, she held a small bowl of freshly ground coffee. I can still remember the scent of the coffee mixing with the spring air.

Taking the brush from my hand she dipped the brush into the bowl and began brushing the collars and cuffs of the coats with the coffee.

"Why are you doing that, Mama?" I asked.

"To clean the oils off the neck and the cuffs," she replied matter-of-factly.

I watched as she vigorously brushed the coffee into the coat collars, shook off the remaining grounds and handed me each clean coat to be taken back into the house.

I'm sure this experience added to my lifelong love affair with coffee. Each fall as the horrible mothball-scented coats were pulled from the closet, I tried to concentrate on the wonderful scent of coffee that would eventually return to them.

Times have changed. No one cleans their coats with coffee now, and few people store them with mothballs. Other things have changed as well. Back in the late '60s, offices used carbon paper to make copies instead of photocopiers. At a recent yard sale my husband came across a 1930s employment test for the New York City railroad. It was hand typed, as were all of the employment tests of that time. Even carbon paper wasn't an option then.

In this era of constantly changing technology, we forget that a few things do remain the same. The Bible tells us that God is the same God he was before the beginning of time. God's love for us and his perfect character remain unchanged as well.

grace by the cup

It comforts me to know that whether coats are refreshed with ground coffee or at the dry cleaners, I can depend on my God to remain the same.

"For I the LORD do not change; therefore you, O sons of Jacob, are not consumed."

Malachi 3:6 RSV

128

50

accountability

Icontinued to sip my iced coffee while feigning a concerted interest in the rather dull artwork offered by the doctor's waiting room. My attention, however, was completely focused on the conversation taking place to my left.

"I just can't believe that Ryan didn't break his arm," said the mother of a child just returning from X-ray.

"Well, it's good that he didn't . . . right?" asked a second woman who was obviously an acquaintance of hers. She added an encouraging smile and a pat on the arm for good measure.

"I guess so," the mother snorted in response to the kind gesture. "The doctor seems to feel it's only bruised, but I'm suing in any case."

"Suing?"

"Ryan hurt his arm on someone else's property."

"Oh! How did it happen?" the friend asked, peering politely over her magazine.

"You know that small orchard that runs next to our housing development? He was crossing over that property to get to his friend's house when he decided to grab an apple. I guess the better ones were high up, so he climbed the tree but couldn't hang on. He fell out of the tree and hurt his arm."

My sideways glance at the pair revealed that the mother had a strangely satisfied smirk on her face. The second woman stared with what can only be described as a look of confusion.

"So, Ryan was climbing a tree on someone else's property. Do you know the guy who owns the orchard?"

"No . . ."

"Did you tell Ryan he could cross this guy's property?"

"No, of course not . . ."

"Were there 'No Trespassing' signs?"

"Well, sure . . . but boys will be boys, you know! The owner should have had a fence up to stop kids from climbing his trees," the mother huffed, snapping her fashion magazine shut with perfectly manicured fingernails.

The tight-lipped expression of her friend revealed that she now understood more than she wanted to.

"So let me see if I've got this right. Ryan was on someone else's property, without permission, and taking fruit that didn't belong to him when he fell out of the tree. Now you think the owner of the property should pay Ryan's medical bills?"

Adjusting a strand of her perfectly coiffed hair, the mother scoffed, "You make it sound like getting hurt was Ryan's fault! He's just a ten-year-old kid. If the owner of the orchard had kid-proofed his property, I would not have had to take off from work to have Ryan's arm x-rayed."

Just then the receptionist called my name. As I watched my son's smiling teenage face come down the hall, I could not decide if I wanted to laugh or to cry. My young man was as responsible a child as any mother could want. Last summer he volunteered at our church's senior citizen program and at a number of its youth programs — while working two jobs to pay for his car and upcoming college expenses. For a young seventeen-year-old he is about as responsible as you could get.

Sure, he makes some bad choices now and then. Don't we all? But when my child was young and he stepped over the line, consequences were swift and sure. His father and I held him accountable for his actions. I think that is one of the keys to growing our children into healthy adults—accountability. I wonder if the mother who was suing the orchard owner understood just what she was teaching her child.

Although I don't care for God's reprimand while it is being administered to me, I am glad that my heavenly Father cares enough about me to apply discipline when it is necessary. He lets the consequences of my actions sting just enough to keep me from falling into the same trap a second time.

And you have forgotten the exhortation that addresses you as children — "My child, do not regard lightly the discipline of the Lord, or lose heart when you are punished by him; for the Lord disciplines those whom he loves, and chastises every child whom he accepts."

Hebrews 12:5–6

51

blinders

The baby shower was winding down. The expectant mother had grinned from ear to ear as the flood of gifts washed upon her. She'd been blessed with everything from an exquisite homemade baby blanket with dainty matching booties to a high-tech, motion-sensitive baby monitoring system.

Now, rubbing her belly and flushed with excitement, the mother-to-be needed to catch her breath while the guests caught up on chitchat.

The guest of honor's sister dutifully passed around coffee and cake. With thirty ladies crowded into a living and dining area not meant for more than a dozen, there was little room to set down a coffee cup. Some opted to balance the cake plate on their knee and hold the cup, while others managed to maneuver the cups under their folding chairs.

The woman seated next to me assessed the situation and wisely decided to call her young daughter to her side.

"Jenny, come sit by me," she called.

Jenny obediently left the grandmotherly women currently doting on her and began to weave her way between the guests toward her mother. I watched as her chubby little legs nearly missed one cup of coffee that was set on the floor, only to bump the knee of a woman holding another cup.

"Jenny, be careful!" the mother called again.

The three-year-old finally arrived at her mother's side and was allowed to nibble on a few bites of her mother's cake. But soon the child's attention moved to the stack of gifts positioned just out of her reach.

When the girl reached for the gifts, her mother gently redirected her hands to the picture book she'd brought with her. The mother reminded the girl that this was her toy and that the others belonged to the new baby. A moment later, forgetting her mother's words, the child was again attracted to the brightly colored baby toys just out of her reach.

After the third reprimand, the woman pulled the child into her lap. She ever so gently cupped her hands on either side of the child's face, then brought her own face down close to the child's.

"Jenny, I said no. You must stay here. The ladies have hot cups of coffee right now, and you can't be wandering around. Now sit down next to me and we'll look at the pictures in your book until we are ready to go. Okay?"

The mother now had her child's full attention. With hands on either side of her face, there was nowhere to look but directly at her mother. This time the words took effect, and the child happily snuggled next to her mother for the remainder of the party. The gifts, the guests, and even the cake could no longer distract her from the book her mother read. Receiving her mother's full attention with no possibility to look elsewhere had done the trick.

At times I think God needs to put some blinders on his children as well. Worldly possessions and events continually pull our attention away from him and put us in danger of being burned. I imagine we often push his patience to the limit with our short attention spans.

In the end, God is forced to send something into our lives that will focus our attention solely on him. He puts blinders on us for just a little while. The little girl squirmed when her mother first pulled her face to within inches of her own. We struggle initially when our Lord uses illness or unemployment to refocus our attention on him. But if we trust him, just the way the little girl trusted her mother, we know we must obey and relinquish control. The situation does not always change. The little girl never did get to play with those distracting toys, but she did find she was perfectly content snuggling alongside the one who kept her safe.

The name of the LORD is a strong tower; the righteous run into it and are safe.

Proverbs 18:10

52

not fair!

I'd just begun making a cup of French press coffee when a friend stopped by the house in need of some consolation. A prestigious honor that truly should have come to him had instead gone to someone else.

"It's just not fair," the young man said. His eyes reflected the hurt that echoed in his voice.

I began to respond with one of the many platitudes that people offer at times such as this but instead forced myself to remain silent. "Nobody ever said life was fair," "Every cloud has a silver lining," and "It's always darkest before the dawn" came to mind faster than I thought possible. They were curtly and rightfully dismissed.

I watched silently and helplessly as this young adult with a boy's broken heart sat before me. With his face in his hands he struggled not to weep, sinking fast into the disappointment that enveloped his world. I listened, prayed, and offered my condolences. We talked about God's goodness, his faithful presence and abundant provision. Then we turned ourselves over to the one who understands even what we don't. I think my friend left my presence comforted, but I knew there would be a scar from this deep wound.

Why does God use tragedy to teach us? I can only look into my own life to answer that question. I am the most compassionate when I relate another person's troubles to my own. I work the hardest for a cause that has hit those I deeply love. I pray more fervently for individuals who share my personal thread of pain. Could God not use joy to bring about the same end? I wonder if Christians would aid their besieged non-Christian friends if Christians always lived happy and carefree lives. When I am riding on a cloud of good fortune, I usually don't see or feel anything but my own pleasure. Not exactly the sympathetic person an ailing coworker might need.

After my young friend left, I returned to making my coffee. If you like fresh, strong coffee, a French press will make you an excellent cup. As I scooped the grounds into the carafe, the coarsely ground coffee dusted my hand. For this particular coffeemaker, the coffee needs to be roughly milled. I noted the texture of the granules as I brushed them off my hand. Each was hard and uneven. I joined the hot water to the coffee grounds and stirred. The clear water changed to a rich shade of brown. Next I inserted the plunger and the lid. Turning the spout away from me, I gently but firmly applied pressure to the plunger. Too much pressure and the coffee would shoot out of the spout; too little pressure and the plunger would stick. When the procedure was complete, I removed the lid, stirred, and started the pressure all over.

As I performed my ritual, it reminded me of life's trials. God applies just the right amount of pressure to produce an excellent person. If we choose to balk at the process and refuse the pressure applied, he may have to start over. I'm sure the coffee beans would prefer to avoid both the grinding and the hot water, but without both, the beans have little purpose.

Life may not be fair, but God is always good.

No fear of me need terrify you; my pressure will not be heavy on you.

Job 33:7

53

plant fertilizer

When I was a young child, my mother never threw out any fruit or vegetable scraps. Potato peels, apple cores, and coffee grounds were all recycled long before local government mandated recycling tin cans and newspapers. We called our recycling process the compost pile.

A friend of mine was recently having some trouble with her outdoor plants and wanted me to accompany her on a lunchtime jaunt to pick up plant fertilizer.

"Why not just throw your coffee grounds around the base of the plants?" I suggested.

"Huh?" she responded, almost raising her eyebrows to the point of no return.

"Those plants need acidic soil. Coffee grounds are acidic and would do the job just as well as some expensive fertilizer. We used to do it all the time when I was a kid."

"Really?"

"Trust me on this. Just wait until the grounds cool and then toss them around the base of the plant. If you don't like the look, mix it with a little dirt and then water the plants. You'll see."

"Well . . . okay . . ."

Weeks later I again saw my friend. She was grinning from ear to ear and waving me to come toward her.

"Let me buy you a cup of coffee," she offered.

"The coffee here is free, hon . . . but thanks for the thought."

Her grin spread farther. "I know it's free! It's just an expression . . . I want to talk to you."

"Oh," I quipped smartly.

"Remember what you told me about the coffee grounds?"

"Yes," I said.

"It worked! The plants are thriving like crazy." Now her eyebrows knit together like a caterpillar as she began to fill the air with questions. "How often should I give them the coffee grounds? Is it better to mix it with the soil or just put it on top of the ground? Is it okay if the grounds actually touch the plant stem? How much water should I give the plants when I put the coffee down?"

"Whoa! This is coffee we're talking about, not some scientifically concocted megagrowth formula. Just throw some under the plants after you are done with your weekend pot of coffee. Water them if you want . . . or wait for the rain. This isn't rocket science."

I returned to my desk amazed at this woman's concern for her plants. I honestly don't have much of a green thumb. My father can grow anything, anywhere. He actually grew a tropical passion plant in Maine—outdoors! I, on the other hand, have trouble growing any plant that is not a weed. Maybe it's because I don't have a compost pile and I don't fertilize the way my dad did. Everyone knows that "rich soil" is good for plants, but few people want to think about what goes into that soil to make it rich. Garbage is something people usually avoid, but what appears to be smelly and offensive isn't always harmful, and plants aren't the only things that need fertilizing.

My life would not be the same if God did not send a little rich refuse my way. Those carefully saved apple cores known as financial struggles, that heap of vegetable peels called physical adversity, and that big scoop of coffee grounds also known as personality conflicts do wonders to alter my stunted growth. God needs to fertilize my life so that it will mature and produce fruit. Once developed, my life can provide nourishment for others, and who knows, God might even let me become fertilizer for someone else's life.

You will be made rich in every way so that you can be generous on every occasion, and through us your generosity will result in thanksgiving to God.

2 Corinthians 9:11 NIV

54

choices

"But, *Mom* . . . *all* the kids have them now!" Stephanie whined.

Keeping her eyes fixed on her coffee cup, my friend Lenora, the girl's mother, took a sip before speaking. "Stephanie, we'll talk about this later."

"But I've just *got* to have a cell phone," Stephanie continued before shifting to a different approach. "Just think, you can call me anywhere. It won't matter if I'm at the mall or at Kelly's house. I could even pick up stuff for you on my way home . . . and when you're gonna be late from work, you don't have to worry about the phone being busy. All you have to do is leave a message with the cell service. Great, huh?"

I watched as my friend braced once again for what was apparently an ongoing battle. Her lips were taut with restraint as she turned away. For the moment it seemed better that she not respond.

Oblivious to the tension, the girl plunged on. "So, Mom? What do you think? Kelly told me about this great deal that —"

At her daughter's persistence, my friend could no longer contain herself. She spun around and flung a look that froze the poor girl in her tracks. Quietly, but with unmistakable resolve, my friend spoke. "Stephanie, if you so much as mention a cell phone again, I'm going to deal out a punishment that will make military school look like a spa vacation. It's not like we haven't talked about this before. You are not, I repeat *not*, going to get a cell phone. Number one, we can't afford it right now, and two, your grades aren't anywhere near what they should be — so I'm not giving you something that is going to take more time away from your homework." My friend paused for just a moment, then added one final point. "And three — you know better than to use the lame excuse 'everyone has one.' Everyone does *not* have one. And even if everyone in the whole world *did* have one, that alone would not justify my getting one for *you*."

Her daughter bit her lip. She appeared tempted to respond but apparently thought better of it.

"I'm sorry, Mom," was all she offered before turning from the kitchen. I caught just a hint of fire left in her eyes and the suggestion of a pout on her teenage lips as she bound up the steps to her bedroom. She may have lost this battle, but I could see that the war was far from over.

Lenora sighed. "I just can't seem to get it through her head that we're broke. When Dennis was laid off last year, things got tight. The job he has now is great, but we still have bills to catch up on." She took a sip of her coffee but had difficulty swallowing over the lump in her throat.

"Good coffee," I offered lamely as I too swallowed some, hoping to give her a moment to recover.

"Oh yes!" Lenora replied quickly. "This is from the gourmet shop in the mall. Carol, the one who is in the choir with me, she says she only buys this brand."

"Isn't it expensive?" I asked, wondering if I was having this conversation with the same person who just told me how tight money was in their household.

"Oh, sure," she quipped, "but it tastes so much better than all the others, doesn't it?"

"Well . . . I, uh, think it's good . . ." I stammered, stirring the spoon nervously around my black coffee. "But to tell you the truth, I know of a few others that taste almost as good for about half the price."

Placing the spoon down on the saucer, I lifted a quick prayer and decided to continue with my thought. "Lenora, do you think that buying expensive coffee is really the way God wants you to use your limited resources right now? Think about what you just told your daughter. You don't want her to have a cell phone simply because her friends have one, but you are buying some pretty overpriced coffee just because someone you know is spending their money on it."

Lenora stared at me wide-eyed. "But . . . it's just that . . ." Then she paused, took a deep breath, and grabbed my hand. "You are right . . . absolutely right. Let's pray together. I need some help to get my priorities straight again. Thanks."

I breathed a sigh of thanks to God for his grace, and we bowed our heads.

For the love of money is a root of all kinds of evil, and in their eagerness to be rich some have wandered away from the faith and pierced themselves with many pains.

1 Timothy 6:10

55

with cream
and sugar, please

W ould you like a cup of coffee?" I heard the receptionist
ask the young man waiting for an interview. His new
suit looked as if the tags should still be hanging from the sleeve,
and his obvious discomfort at wearing a shirt and tie made his
right-out-of-college haircut all the more obvious.

"Thank you, I would," he replied, unconsciously straight-
ening his tie. I was not at all certain that coffee would have
been this young man's normal choice. He looked more like a
pizza-and-coke-for-breakfast kind of guy. I smiled to myself
as I finished gathering my paperwork.

"How would you like that?" the receptionist called over her
shoulder as she headed down the hall.

"Cream and two sugars," he called after her.

I was just about to leave when she popped her head around
the corner and said, "I'm sorry, but someone used the last of
the cream. Is that okay?"

He smiled and told her that just sugar would be fine.

A split second after that she again appeared and apologetically announced, "Apparently we have no sugar left either. All I can offer you is black coffee."

As nervous as the fellow was, he just took it all in stride. "Actually, black would be perfect. I need to cut back on the sugar anyway." He smiled pleasantly to assure her that he meant it and waited for her to return with the coffee.

Now, I'd just gotten myself a cup of coffee not five minutes before this happened, and I knew that there was both cream and sugar. My curiosity had been piqued, and I decided to find out what was going on.

Motioning the receptionist to follow me, I asked her why she'd told the young man there was no cream or sugar when there really was.

She grinned and offered me this: "There are two people in line for one job opening. Both have been in for interviews before and are equally qualified. The boss wanted to find out which of the two would best deal with difficult clients. I knew both liked their coffee with cream and sugar. When they came in, I kept both waiting for over an hour. Then I offered them coffee but disappointed them when they couldn't have it the way they liked it. I figured whoever handled the situation best would be better able to deal with some client who wanted everything his or her way."

I stared openmouthed for just a moment, then asked the obvious question. "I saw how the kid handled it, but what about the other guy?"

"Well . . . to tell you the truth, I figured the other guy would handle it better than the kid did. He was older, and usually age produces some maturity. Didn't happen that way though. The older guy was obviously annoyed that he was kept waiting for an hour. When I told him we didn't have cream, he became rather curt and told me I could add an extra sugar. When I returned the second time and told him we had no sugar, he grumbled something under his breath. I told the boss to pick the kid."

Returning to my desk, I sent an encouraging smile to the young man still waiting in the reception area. He grinned back, still nervous but not unpleasant. It made me wonder how I would have reacted in the same situation.

Paul and Silas certainly showed what mettle they were made of while enduring much harsher circumstances. They did not allow imprisonment and life's adversities to discourage or immobilize them. Singing praises to God and praying for their captors eventually brought the jailer and his whole family to know the joy of salvation.

Sometimes it is not our surroundings, our tools, or our talents that inspire others . . . it is our attitude.

At midnight Paul and Silas were praying and singing hymns to God.

Acts 16:25 NKJV

56

beauty

Unable to sit still, I repositioned myself in the slick salon chair for the hundredth time. Waiting for anything is not easy for me, but waiting without the ability to stretch my legs is even worse. Setting aside a rather dated magazine, I decided to amuse myself by indulging in one of my favorite pastimes — people watching.

The beauty salon was filled with a variety of interesting people. Teenage girls sat in a number of the chairs. For some strange reason they seemed to think that their trim bodies, quick minds, and "cute as a button" noses did not make them perfect enough. The latest hair colors and cuts were being weighed among them with great care, and no doubt they were enjoying the whole process.

Being that it was Saturday, a number of career-minded women were in the salon. Perfection seemed the order of the day for them as well, but I did notice that this group spent less time browsing through the stylebooks and that they were quick to point their perfectly manicured fingers at any strand that was not handled with utmost care.

Watching the comings and goings around me, I wondered where I fell into this mix. I was certainly no teenager, and unlike some of the professionals being coiffed, my bills required that most of my paycheck be applied to more mundane things. I did notice, however, that the young girls and the educated professionals had one thing in common — they were giving the orders.

"Here, let me take that," offered my hairdresser, taking my cold cup of coffee with one hand as she checked the status of the highlighting chemical with her other. "I think we're ready," she smiled, knowing my impatient nature.

Peg, the woman I sought out when my tresses became unmanageable, is a living doll. She knows exactly what I want. Short, but not boyish. Simple, but not plain. I'm just not the type to fuss with my hair, so it has to be low maintenance. Peg occasionally suggests small changes but never asks me to jump into a pool of thick mousse or join the glow-in-the-dark generation. I like her approach.

Finding a stylist who would accept my unwillingness to fuss was a challenge. For a few years I even resorted to shoulder-length hair that required no professional touch. Each month I would coerce my dear husband to take scissors to the back of my locks and I would gingerly trim the sides. Needless to say, this produced less than stellar results.

Finally, with the irrevocable insistence of my spouse, I began my search for a compatible stylist. It took a few awful haircuts by overzealous stylists, but eventually I stumbled upon Peg. I think she knew from the beginning that I needed a major overhaul, but she never pushed too fast. Each month she would suggest one little change — a shorter cut, a few highlights, or a new styling technique. My hair is now easier to care for, quicker to style, and without a doubt more attractive.

Peg's gentle manner and her willingness to listen to my needs made me eager to hear her suggestions. I don't particularly like change, but I am now happy to place myself in her more than capable hands. Peg has experience and a real sense of style that I don't. When I approach a new Christian friend with advice,

I try to think of Peg. First, I must earn their trust by listening to their needs. Only then will I know how to help.

As you know and as God is our witness, we never came with words of flattery or with a pretext for greed; nor did we seek praise. . . . But we were gentle among you, like a nurse tenderly caring for her own children.

1 Thessalonians 2:5–7

tangles

E ach child seemed to arrive with bounce and a chuckle. From the tiniest preschoolers to the preadolescent sixth graders, it seemed that the young people attending vacation Bible school were looking forward to their evening. I wish I could have said the same about all the adult volunteers. After a long day at the office, some of us were rushing to finish last-minute preparations. Skit props had been mislaid, snacks needed to be set up, and craft projects begged for an organized hand.

A fellow volunteer entered my story room shortly before program time. "We're meeting for prayer down the hall," she stated matter-of-factly.

"Sure, I'll be right with you. Just let me finish getting this ready," I replied with a forced smile.

A moment later the tapping of her foot turned my eyes from the knot of beads I was attempting to untangle. "Why don't you go ahead without me. I just need to —"

My friend gently but firmly removed the beads from my hands. "That can wait. Prayer for the kids *can't* wait. Let's go."

Her hand underneath my elbow, she led me out of the room and down the hall where others already gathered.

"Lord, remind us why we are here . . ." one voice prayed, "and help us set aside those things that clutter our minds, and prepare us to meet the needs of those you send here. Let us hear and learn what you want to teach us, as well as what we are supposed to teach the children."

Entering as quietly as I could, I bowed my head and listened to the prayers lifted by the group. But my mind kept returning to the tangle of beads in my story room.

". . . allow us to have Martha's hands but Mary's heart," the voice continued.

"Mary's heart," I echoed absentmindedly.

"Amen."

The group dispersed, and I trudged back to my jumble of chains, frustration mounting with each step.

"You okay?" my friend asked, again popping her head into the room.

"Sure," I replied unenthusiastically.

Without invitation she plopped herself down at the foot of my colored pool and asked, "Need some help with these?"

"I don't know if it will do any good, but you are welcome to try," I grumbled.

While our fingers nimbly untangled the strands together, we chatted. Only minutes passed before the strings lay in neat rows on the table.

"Thanks," I offered somewhat sheepishly. With the problem solved, I found myself once again looking forward to the children's arrival.

She grinned broadly and stated the obvious. "All you needed was a little help."

Asking for help is not my strong suit, but I dare not let my problems keep me from God's presence. Martha had to be rebuked by Jesus because she was putting her worries before her worship (Luke 10:39–42). I would prefer to be like Mary. As Christians we can help other believers make the best use of their time. This may mean taking them by the hand and leading them down the hall to pray, or it might mean filling the stomach of a hungry child so that his mother can hear Jesus' words of comfort. I have found that it is never enough to simply tell others what to do. The best lessons come from those who pray first, then are willing to roll up their sleeves and turn out their pockets.

Nevertheless you have done well that you shared in my distress.

Philippians 4:14 NKJV

58

nearness

I heard my footsteps' hollow echo on the floor as I crossed our deserted church basement. In the kitchen I rinsed the coffeepot, cleared away crumpled napkins, disposed of half-eaten slivers of cake, and purged stale beverages from their Styrofoam containers. Finishing up the last of my tasks, I breathed a weary sigh and turned off the lights.

The warmth of my last cup of coffee had long since gone, and the whisper of a cold autumn wind sent a chill up my spine as I locked the church door behind me. Headlights bored through the darkness as I drove into the clear cold evening, eager to rest my body and bask in the nurture of my family. But this was not to be. Members of my family had either retired for the night or settled into the rhythm of their own evening routines. The only living creature to greet me was my cat, Einstein. He strolled across the room with his usual regal bearing and granted me the pleasure of a brush along my ankle and an almost soundless "Meow."

Too wound up to sleep and too tired to work, I chose to settle in for a bit of quiet time. My workday had been particularly grueling and the church meeting not particularly productive.

The day's tension begged for release, but I did not want to burden my family with a tedious rendition of its trials. Armed with a good book and a warm quilt, and no phone to divert my attention, I propped a few pillows up against the headboard of my bed and tried to relax.

I'd just turned the first page when Einstein sauntered into my bedroom looking for attention. He did not know or care about my difficult day. He simply wanted to share my company. I tried to ignore him as he jumped onto the bed and positioned his nose under my arm, nudging me and rubbing his face against my hand hoping for a caress. When he received only a cursory pat, his approach became decidedly more aggressive. His head now wedged itself under my book, and his front paws gingerly placed themselves on my chest. Before I knew it, he'd stretched himself full length along my body, his chin resting against my cheek and his eyes staring into mine. His whiskers tickled the side of my face unmercifully, and when even this did not yield the desired results, a gentle nip on the end of my chin unquestionably wrenched my attention from the book I was reading to his determined silver and white face.

I began stroking his sleek gray fur and was immediately rewarded for my endeavor. His body relaxed under my hand, his paws curling themselves gently beneath his breast as he tucked his chin into the resulting crevice. The sound of his contented purring made me smile. As my fingers yielded to Einstein's soft warm coat, I could feel the tension of the day tumble away while peace filled its void. Einstein wanted to be with me. Dirty coffee cups, cold winter winds, and misplaced accounting reports all disappeared in that deep-throated hum. By filling his need, my need was taken care of as well. If a creature as unpretentious as a cat can provide companionship in a moment of stress, imagine our pleasure when we spend time with our Creator—the one who loved us more than his own life.

But for me it is good to be near God.

Psalm 73:28

59

expectations

Only a good cup of java would properly cap off the fun and laughter of this late evening. When our hostess offered her guests the option, I could feel a satisfied grin spread across my face. My friends continued to chat and I basked in the warmth of their company—until I took the first sip of my beverage. I expected the silky taste of rich black coffee and instead sampled the bite of orange pekoe tea. Somehow the wrong beverage had been placed in front of me. Because I was so wrapped up in my own agenda, I took my first sip without noticing the tea packet alongside the cup.

Life brims with the unexpected. My sister, Helga, discovered this reality shortly after her daughter was born. A near-textbook pregnancy did not result in the healthy child she expected. Little Erica's kidneys and bladder had not developed normally. Two major surgeries were required during the first precious week of her life. Twenty more surgeries were scheduled over the next ten years. A single parent, my sister relinquished job after job, because she was unable to leave Erica's hospital bed for weeks at a time. A car held together with little more than spit and chewing gum, frequent relocations to better access special hospital facilities, and numerous trips to food banks and thrift shops took their toll on my sister's self-reliance. Helga found herself facing the question asked by so many in ages past: "Why me?" Helga's dreams of a healthy daughter and a perfect family had disappeared as quickly as a summer rain in the desert sand.

Shortly after Erica's birth, Helga vented her pain, frustration, and disappointment through periods of weeping and praying. Most nights were spent in hard-backed hospital chairs, her arms wrapped about her body in an attempt to suppress their emptiness. Her heart wrenched with every gaze at the tubes taped to her tiny incubated infant. Things were not supposed to turn out this way. She begged God to heal her daughter, but no miracles occurred, and the endless stream of medical procedures continued to press on her spirit. Then a conversation with my father brought Helga to a new mind-set. She asked my dad what was to become of her dreams for the future. Dad, no less torn by the difficulties his daughter and new granddaughter were going through, responded with evidence of a faith that had overcome many challenging circumstances. "When your dreams die, you stand strong and pick up a new set of dreams," he said.

Erica is now a "normal" teenage girl. Physically, emotionally, and spiritually, she still faces challenges other teens do not, but her childhood was filled with her mother's unending love and God's mercy. When I recently asked Helga about her dreams for the future, she responded with a laugh.

"My dreams don't always come true, but God's plans for me are always better than my dreams. My faith is stronger than it ever was, and I now realize that Erica was *exactly* the daughter I needed to get me where I am today. She was the perfect daughter for me. I have a big smooth rock in my backyard garden. I recently painted these words on it '*Be happy with what you have. Rejoice in the way things are. When you realize there is nothing lacking, then the world is yours.'* Every morning I read those words to remind me that I really do have everything I need."

Helga's current dream is to buy a small house and provide a college education for Erica. Unless God works a miracle, these dreams may never become a reality, but Helga knows that God will not let go of her hand, no matter how rough the path she must walk.

"For I, the Lord your God, hold your right hand; it is I who say to you, 'Do not fear, I will help you.'"

Isaiah 41:13

60

the end

The small brown ring remaining at the bottom of my mug seemed to beg for company, but time did not permit me a second cup of coffee. The day was cold, windy, and bleak. Nothing made more sense than refilling my mug with a favorite beverage, grabbing a warm quilt, and curling up with a good book in a quiet house. Instead I was off to one of my least favorite places—a crowded shopping mall on a Saturday afternoon.

The old adage "All good things must come to an end" sprang to mind as I put the car in gear and headed out. God must have been preparing me for the day ahead, because it wasn't long before I hit a sluggish, post-holiday detour. Traffic crawled along, the street crew directed cars, and I reflected on how many things take our lives off the easy road.

An old factory closes its rust-encrusted doors, but a job retraining program provides fresh and unexpected opportunities for the laid-off employees. Tears flow freely when a dear friend moves away, but delight shows its face when the one left behind discovers a like-minded neighbor interested in gardening. The deep winter snow plants seeds of unrest in an elderly housebound gentleman until he shares his colorful stamp collection with the young boy who shovels his walkway. Change is inevitable, sometimes difficult, but never inherently bad.

I've watched my three boys grow from knee-scraped toddlers into strapping teenagers, then stretch themselves farther to become perceptive young men. Moving from one stage to another with them was frequently challenging, often rewarding, but seldom easy. No one wants to take the detour set in his or her path, and few people enjoy foregoing that second cup of coffee in order to traipse out into the cold. However, refusing change is like a pond refusing the freshwater coming from its spring. Without the pond's source, the water becomes stagnant and dead. It is better to accept the new water than to fight it.

Yes, all things, good and bad, do come to an end. There is a time and season for each item and event in history. Embrace God's creation and his changes knowing that he has only the best in store for you.

When you turn the last page of a good book, God is ready to supply you with another. Do not lament the ending. Rejoice in the new adventure to come.

There is a time for everything and a season for every activity under heaven: a time to be born and a time to die, a time to plant and a time to uproot, a time to kill and a time to heal, a time to tear down and a time to build, a time to weep and a time to laugh, a time to mourn and a time to dance, a time to scatter stones and a time to gather them, a time to embrace and a time to refrain, a time to search and a time to give up, a time to keep and a time to throw away, a time to tear and a time to mend, a time to be silent and a time to speak, a time to love and a time to hate, a time for war and a time for peace.

Ecclesiastes 3:1–8 NIV

Louise Bergmann DuMont has written for numerous periodicals, journals, and newspapers and is the facilitator of the North Jersey Christian Writers' Group. A wife and mother of three grown boys, she often uses everyday experiences to fuel her writing. Her Internet columns, "Coffee And . . ." and "Coffee Nips," can be found at www.crosshome.com and www.ringwoodbaptist.org.